A Guide to
Illinois
Nature Centers
& Interpretive
Trails

Walter G. Zyznieuski
and George S. Zyznieuski

A Guide to

Illinois Nature Centers & *Interpretive Trails*

Southern
Illinois
University
Press
Carbondale
and
Edwardsville

Library of Congress Cataloging-in-Publication Data
Zyznieuski, Walter.
   A guide to Illinois nature centers and interpretive trails / Walter G.
Zyznieuski and George S. Zyznieuski.
       p.   cm.
   Includes bibliographical references and index.
   1. Nature centers—Illinois—Guidebooks.   2. Nature trails—
Illinois—Guidebooks.   3. Illinois—Guidebooks.   I. Zyznieuski,
George, date.   II. Title.
QH76.5.I5 Z98 2002
   796.5—dc21

                                                    2001042645

ISBN 0-8093-2430-X

Printed on recycled paper. ♻

The paper used in this publication meets the minimum
requirements of American National Standard for Information
Sciences—Permanence of Paper for Printed Library Materials,
ANSI Z39.48-1992. ∞

To our families —
Deb, Nicholas,
and Douglas
Laura and Elisha

The country of the Illinois enjoys all advantages—not only beauty, but also a plenitude of all things needed to support human life. The prairie, which is watered by the river, is beautified by small hills covered with groves of oaks and walnut trees. The prairies are full of grass, growing very tall.

—Joutel, a French soldier, 1684–85
(from William Joseph Seno, *Up Country*)

Contents

Central Illinois

Southern Illinois

Illustrations

Preface

Writing a book on Illinois's nature centers and interpretive trails was a unique learning experience for us. Growing up in Chicago allowed us the opportunity to explore the numerous trails and the long distance trail network throughout the forest preserves and associated greenways of that region. As we went away to college in other parts of Illinois, we continued our outdoor recreational pursuits throughout the state. Our subsequent explorations, carried out both for fun and for publication purposes, made us aware of yet more fascinating recreational and educational family activities and opportunities along interpretive trails and at nature centers. That research has led to the writing of this book. Although we were familiar with many of the trails and nature centers in the state and what they offer, every time we visited one of them we learned something else about the flora and fauna found there, the history and geology of the site, the Native Americans who once called the area home, or how the climate played a part in shaping the place. We have seen many sites where once-productive fields are being restored to presettlement prairies, revealing how the Prairie State used to look. We were impressed by many individuals, groups, organizations, parks, and interpretive centers that are creating and managing these sites for future generations. We applaud their efforts and encourage more municipalities, parks, other organizations (both public and private), and individuals to plant a prairie or wildflower garden, build a short trail system, or provide some interpretive signs for the public to read and enjoy.

Although much of Illinois consists of urbanized, populated centers and highly cultivated farmland, the state does have many significant ecological, archaeological, historical, and wild areas—and we were able to capture many of them in *Illinois Nature Centers and Interpretive Trails*. Our focus in this book is on short nature and interpretive trails that families with young children, elderly individuals, or people with disabilities would be able to enjoy. Also covered are nature centers that feature programs and exhibits as well as nature trails. Each year, millions of Americans want to get away from the hustle and bustle of everyday life and explore nature. Many of the trails and parks found in Illinois are isolated ecological "islands" that offer the perfect getaway. For example, the North Park Village Nature Center on the North Side of Chicago, near where we grew up, is an excellent urban nature education center and associated trail system created by the Chicago Department of Environment. We encourage those individuals who are not familiar with what nature has to offer in their own backyards or around the state to pick one of the locations in this book and then go explore that site.

In researching these sites, we were pleasantly surprised at what the combination of nature and human effort presented along the trail: spectacular displays of wildflowers, restored prairies, old growth forests, and numerous bird species, including wild turkeys taking off in flight, trumpeter swans visiting a wildlife preserve, and hundreds of migrating snow geese flying overhead. We enjoyed observing a red fox coming down the trail towards us; spying a newly born copperhead; reviewing an interpretive sign describing a feature of the site; following an interpretive trail along an old steel mill foundation; hiking along the historic Illinois and Michigan Canal and associated locks; exploring the area where Joliet and Marquette passed through at the Chicago Portage; viewing unusual old rock formations; finding pieces of chert that had been chipped by a Native American; and uncovering fossils. We brought along our family members on many of the outings to enjoy nature up close and firsthand and were pleased to see the thrill on their faces as we walked through a prairie where butterflies circled us, found a turtle along the trail, participated in a guided nature hike, reviewed a nature exhibit or trail sign, or tried to identify a set of animal tracks, a wildflower, or a tree. Many times, we used a stroller or a child carrier along trails or at nature centers. Many of the nature and interpretive trails are fairly short, are relatively easy to hike and explore, and require that only a little equipment be carried, making them enjoyable family adventures.

Although in writing this book we attempted to find, explore, and write about as many nature centers and interpretive trails in Illinois as we could, we realize that we may have excluded others. We regret not being able to include all of them in our statewide coverage. We hope that readers will take the opportunity to visit at least some of the trails or nature centers described here. Each trail has unique features, and there are outstanding displays, hands-on exhibits, and programs available at many nature centers. We hope to see you out along one of the trails or at a nature center, enjoying Illinois's natural wonders with us.

Acknowledgments

We wish to thank the many individuals who helped us with this book. First of all, we thank our families (Deb, Nicholas, and Douglas Zyznieuski and Mary Ann, Marty, and Lindsay Anderson) for joining us on hikes and visiting nature centers around the state. We hope that the trail experiences, wildlife encounters, and prairie scenes, as well as nature exhibits, will stay with them a lifetime. We also thank a few friends who joined us on the trails, including the family of Gary Stratton and Greg and Tom Feeny.

Many park naturalists and other staff were extremely helpful in providing park information and maps. We especially thank Jim Matheis of Lincoln Memorial Garden and Nature Center for reviewing our trail write-up and providing us with the latest trail map; Dave Nance of Anderson Prairie Park for information on that beautiful prairie restoration site; and Carol Thompson, staff naturalist at Weldon Springs State Recreation Area, for giving us a tour of the nature center and school and providing us with park information and for her dedication in undertaking naturalist activities at the park. Thanks also to Susan Allen for reviewing our text. Special thanks to our parents, Anna and Nick, for watching our sons during our hikes, for the great meals, and for the roof over our heads.

We also thank park staff and staff naturalists around the state for their guided nature walks and for explaining the flora and fauna and natural history of the sites to us. We especially thank Philip Vierling for an excellent tour of the Chicago Portage National Historic Site and for his initial call for the development of a visitor center there. Because of his perseverance, and with help and coordination from other organizations, it appears likely that a visitor center for this historic site will become a reality in the future.

Finally, we thank Southern Illinois University Press and its staff, especially Jim Simmons, for encouraging us on the initial concept and believing in our work, and Karl Kageff, for working closely and diligently with us to produce the final result.

Introduction

This guidebook describes 132 locations throughout Illinois, including nature centers and associated trails; designated nature trails found at nature preserves and other parks; trails that are designated accessible for people with disabilities, families, or the elderly; and trails that are designed to be interpretive (most are self-guided). We do not describe many paved bicycle trails, unless they were designated specifically as accessible. The accessible trails are generally level, and the trail surface may consist of concrete or asphalt, dirt, or packed gravel. The key to sites map shows the locations of all 132 sites, starting from the northwest part of the state down to the far southern counties. The book itself is divided into three parts, covering northern, central, and southern Illinois.

In addition to those covered in this book, numerous other hiking trails are also to be found at Illinois state parks, the Shawnee National Forest, wildlife refuges, municipal parks, and other locations. The federal government recently set aside 19,000 acres south of Chicago for the Midewin National Tallgrass Prairie, which will offer numerous outdoor recreation activities in the future. In addition, the Cache River State Natural Area and the Cypress Creek National Wildlife Refuge in southern Illinois are home to numerous threatened and endangered species and outstanding natural features, and they have many areas to explore. Various organizations are in the process of buying additional properties along the Cache River complex in order to enlarge and protect a unique natural resource. In central Illinois, the 30,000-acre Jim Edgar Panther Creek State Fish and Wildlife Area offers trails to explore and other recreation activities. Also, a regional group of organizations is promoting outstanding natural lands (wetlands, woodlands, and prairies), stretching from southeastern Wisconsin to northeastern Illinois and northwestern Indiana, known as the Chicago Wilderness. Numerous opportunities to explore some of these areas are available, and a few of these sites are included in this book.

The trails and nature centers described in this book may be enjoyed by families, groups, and individuals of all ages and activity levels. By the term *nature center*, we refer to visitor centers, interpretive centers, education centers, learning centers, and museums, as well as facilities that identify themselves as nature centers. Also included in many of the site descriptions are the titles of programs sponsored by the particular nature center or park. Our intention was to identify some of the most popular programs; however, readers may find other programs listed in catalogs or newsletters. Often, a small fee is charged for the programs.

As with our previous trail books, we personally toured each site, hiked the trails, visited the nature centers, and conversed with many staff or park personnel to learn about the trails and other features of the site. Some information was obtained from park brochures or other sources. Included in the contact information for each nature center or park are the Web sites of the organizations, if available. The appendix contains additional Web sites, addresses, and phone numbers of related organizations such as the Illinois Department of Natural Resources, which maintains a Web page for all state parks.

Although the information provided in this book is current at the time of writing, changes do occur, and it is always wise to contact the site prior to visiting. For those who are looking for greater challenges in trail length, difficulty, or diversity or who simply want more information, please refer to our *Guide to Mountain Bike Trails in Illinois* and *Illinois Hiking and Backpacking Trails*, revised edition. In this book, we include a representative sample of maps from the parks or the trail organizations; so the legends and keys differ somewhat from map to map and from the list of symbols that follow this introduction. In many cases, a trail map or guide is available at the trailhead or from the trail entity. We also include many photographs taken while hiking along the trail or exploring a nature center.

Although nature and interpretive trails tend to be shorter in length than backpacking trails, obstacles, hazards, and challenging terrain may still be present. The topography varies from location to location, and depending on the site, the hiker may encounter rivers, stream crossings, overlooks, high cliffs, bluffs, ridges, and other potential dangers. Always contact the site personnel for trail conditions prior to your visit, and take appropriate cautions with friends and family members. Many animals and insects may be seen in the wild while hiking, but if care is taken, the encounters with wildlife will usually be only visual and conflicts can be avoided. There is, however, a potential threat to hikers' health during the warmer months from a common insect known as the deer tick that can transmit Lyme disease, which can cause significant illness. Hikers should take appropriate action, including wearing long pants tucked into socks, long-sleeve shirts, and hats. Also, conduct a complete and thorough check of yourself, your children, and pets after hiking. In addition, poison ivy is found on or along many trails, so keep an eye on your children or others in your group who may be susceptible to a rash from contact with this plant. Finally, we would like to recommend some basic clothing and equipment for parents with children. First, always provide appropriate outerwear for the weather. Rain gear, hats, coats, and good footwear should be checked before leaving home. Children in particular should have appropriate footwear, as well as sunscreen, bug or tick repellent, sunglasses, and a whistle. A small first-aid kit, a water bottle, and snacks come in handy, too. Additional hiking information and suggestions of items to carry may be found in some of the books listed in the selected bibliography, including those by Alice Cary and by Steven A. Griffin and Elizabeth May, as well as our own *Illinois Hiking and Backpacking Trails.* Also see the Illinois Department of Public Health's Web site for additional precautions.

The best way to enjoy these trails and nature centers is to be there! It is our hope that we have provided you with the appropriate information to get you to a place you've never been. Enjoy the nature centers and the interpretive and nature trails of Illinois!

Symbols

The following symbols are used in the site descriptions:

&#9855;	accessible trail	&#127907;	hunting
	bike path		ice skating
	bike rack	**?**	information
	boat launch		in-line skating
▲	camping		interpretive trail
	canoeing		lodging
	concession		park office
	cross-country skiing		picnic area
	drinking water		picnic shelter
	dump station		playground
	first aid		rest rooms
	fishing		sledding
	gift shop		swimming
	hiking trail	**(**	telephone
	horseback riding		wildlife observation area

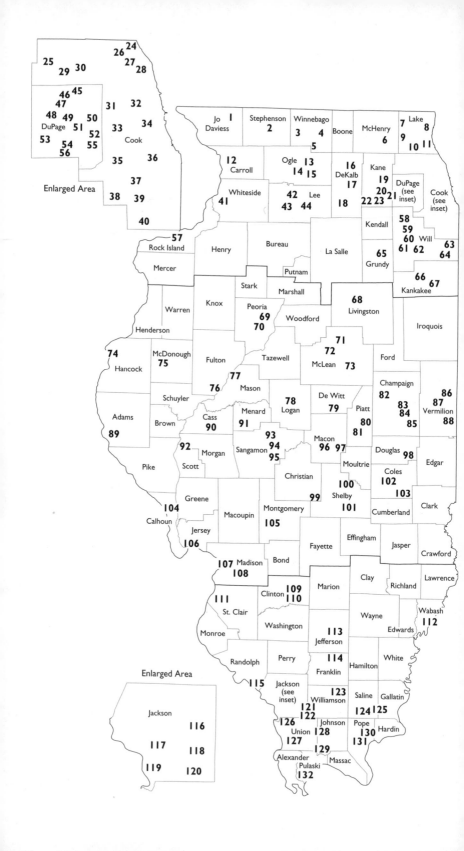

Legend

Northern Illinois

Central Illinois

Northern Illinois

1.   Apple River Canyon State Park

HIGHLIGHTS:
- *Self-guided nature trail*
- *4 additional nature trails*
- *Apple River*
- *Massive cliffs*
- *Colorful canyon*
- *Wildlife, including eagles*

DESCRIPTION: Apple River Canyon State Park is in the hilly northwest part of Jo Daviess County near the Wisconsin border. This scenic canyon was formed by the action of the winding waters of the Apple River. The **Primrose Nature Trail,** named after a tiny spring flower, follows the river along the bluff line. The 1-mile (one way), mostly dirt trail is accessed by a steep wooden stairway along the blacktop road .25 mile west of the Canyon Park Road or between campsites 41 and 42 in the Canyon Ridge camping area. This nature study area is filled with a diversity of plants and wildlife and with exciting views of the river canyon. A descriptive trail brochure is available from the park office. All along the Primrose Trail and the other trails within the park are great views of limestone bluffs, deep ravines, springs, and streams. Late spring and early fall are especially good times to visit.

HOURS: The office is open Monday–Friday, 8:00 AM–4:00 PM. The park is open daily, sunrise to sunset.

DIRECTIONS: From US 20 west of Freeport, take IL 78 north for 6 miles to Canyon Road, turn left (west), and follow it 3.5 miles to the park.

CONTACT INFORMATION: Apple River Canyon State Park, 8763 E. Canyon Rd., Apple River, IL 61001; (815) 745-3302; www.dnr.state.il.us/lands/landmgt/parks/r1/apple.htm

2. Oakdale Nature Preserve

HIGHLIGHTS:
- *Environmental learning center*
- *133-acre nature preserve*
- *5 miles of hiking trails*
- *Restored prairies*

DESCRIPTION: Oakdale Nature Preserve is 3 miles south of Freeport in Stephenson County. It has an environmental learning center with a classroom setting that is used for various outdoor education and special programs. The trail system at Oakdale is made up of 12 connecting loop trails totaling 5 miles. A seasonal trail guide is available from the Freeport Park District. Throughout the preserve, the hiker will find oak and hickory forests as well as various tall grasses of the prairies, shrubs, numerous wildflowers, and many common animals, including deer. Most of the trail itself is mowed grass and dirt. Some of the most challenging sections of the trail system are on the west side of Crane's Grove Road and along Crane's Creek. Also very scenic is the trail section heading south from the preserve buildings; it parallels Crane's Creek and then crosses the creek via a footbridge. Additional trail loops are available west of the bridge; or for the return route, hikers can head east and then turn back north to the preserve parking lot and buildings. The trails at Oakdale can be enjoyed year-round.

REGULATIONS: Remain on trails. Do not remove anything. Pets must be leashed.

HOURS: The park closes at sundown.

DIRECTIONS: From US Business Route 20, which becomes South Street at the southeast part of Freeport, take Baileyville Road south 3 miles. Look for the sign at Crane's Grove Road and turn west to the entrance.

CONTACT INFORMATION: Oakdale Nature Preserve, Freeport Park District, 1200 Park Lane Dr., Freeport, IL 61032; (815) 235-6114 or (815) 233-5616

3. Pecatonica River Forest Preserve

HIGHLIGHTS:
- *Environmental education center*
- *36-acre Illinois Nature Preserve*
- *Prairie restoration project*

PROGRAMS AND EVENTS:
- *Geology*
- *Map and compass use*
- *Edible wild foods*
- *Maple syrup production*
- *Wildflowers*
- *Pioneer life*
- *Animal tracking*
- *Animal habitats*
- *Animals in winter*
- *Migration*
- *Aquatic life*

DESCRIPTION: The Pecatonica River Forest Preserve, northwest of Rockford in Winnebago County, features over 400 acres of forests and fields, along with lakes and the Pecatonica River, all providing home to a variety of plants and animals. The self-guided **Oxbow Lake Trail** has 29 interpretive stations, with post number 1 just south of the flagpole by the Highview Shelter House. The majority of the trail is south and west of Brick School Road/Judd Road, which curves through the preserve, directly south of the stone barn that serves as an environmental education center. The trail is a 1.5-mile loop and consists of dirt and mowed grass. A 27-page nature trail booklet, available at the beginning of the trail, describes the history of the area as well as the plants, aquatic life, and wildlife of the area. From station 7 to station 21, the trail circles around Oxbow Lake and a marsh and parallels the Pecatonica River. This low-lying area can be submerged during periods of high rainfall. Visitors should check with preserve staff for trail conditions ahead of time.

REGULATIONS: Remain on trails. Do not remove anything. Pets must be leashed.

HOURS: The preserve is open daily, sunrise to sunset.

DIRECTIONS: Take IL 70 west out of Rockford 8.5 miles to Judd Road, turn left (south), and continue for 1.5 miles to the sign for the camping area and for Highview Shelter House, where parking is available.

CONTACT INFORMATION: Winnebago County Forest Preserves, 5500 Northrock Dr., Rockford, IL 61103; (815) 877-6100

4.   Klehm Arboretum and Botanic Garden

HIGHLIGHTS:
- *Interpretive trail*
- *Gift shop*
- *Botanical education center*
- *Accessible trail*
- *Exhibits*
- *Membership opportunities*

PROGRAMS AND EVENTS:
- *Children's programs*
- *Guided tours*
- *Botanical education*
- *Lectures*
- *Symposiums*
- *Workshops*
- *Demonstrations*
- *Plant clinics*
- *Winter woods walk*

DESCRIPTION: The Klehm Arboretum and Botanic Garden in southwestern Rockford (Winnebago County) features an outstanding education center for botanical society members as well as for the general public. It holds classes and provides outdoor and botanical information. The Northern Illinois Botanical Society works in partnership with the Winnebago County Forest Preserve to enhance and maintain the facility. A mostly accessible interpretive trail allows the visitor to partake of over 150 acres of trees and other plants, and a helpful interpretive guide is available on site. The trail totals 2 miles, of which 1.5 miles are paved and the rest is a wood-chip path. In all seasons, visitors will encounter unusual trees and other plants not typically found in the Midwest. There are also community gardening areas available.

REGULATIONS: No pets allowed. Stay on trails.

HOURS: The site is open daily, 9:00 AM–4:00 PM.

DIRECTIONS: From US 20 south of Rockford, go 1 mile north on IL 2 (South Main). Turn left on Clifton Avenue and left again into the entrance for the arboretum.

CONTACT INFORMATION: The Klehm Arboretum and Botanic Garden, 2701 Clifton Ave., Rockford, IL 61102; (815) 965-8146 or (888) 419-0782

5.   Severson Dells Forest Preserve

HIGHLIGHTS:
- *Environmental education center*
- *Staff naturalist*
- Notes from the Dells *newsletter*
- *Wildlife sanctuary*
- *Library*
- *Prairie garden*
- *21-acre Illinois Nature Preserve*
- *Limestone cliffs*
- *Membership opportunities*

PROGRAMS AND EVENTS:
- *Reading from the Rookery*
- *Early Morning Bird Walk*
- *Mother's Day Wildflower Walk*
- *Night Skies over Severson*

DESCRIPTION: Severson Dells Forest Preserve is 3.5 miles southwest of Rockford in Winnebago County. The **Severson Dells Self-Guided Nature Trail** begins and ends at the environmental education center. Seasonal trail guide booklets available at the center provide information about the variety of plants in the area. There are 26 numbered stations along the trail. The accessible portion of the loop, consisting of stations 1–6 and 24–26, is asphalt paved and close to the education center; the rest of the trail is dirt. The area features oak and hickory woods, meadow and marshland, a wildlife pond, and Hall Creek. The entire area offers views of wildflowers and plants, including some rare species such as the Green Dragon. One of the highlights is the limestone cliffs and valley known as the Dells (station 19).

HOURS: Trails are open daily, 7:00 AM to sunset; the education center is open Monday–Saturday, 8:00 AM–4:30 PM, and Sunday, 1:00–4:30 PM.

DIRECTIONS: From US 20 south of Rockford, go west on Montague Road for 3.5 miles, past Weldon Road, to the entrance on the south side of the road.

CONTACT INFORMATION: Severson Dells Environmental Education Center, 8786 Montague Rd., Rockford, IL 61102-9703; (815) 335-2915; www.seversondells.org

6. Moraine Hills State Park

HIGHLIGHTS:
- *Nature center*
- *Displays*
- *Staff interpreters*
- *242-acre Illinois Nature Preserve*
- *Fox River*
- *Accessible fishing pier*
- *Lake Defiance self-guided interpretive trail*

PROGRAMS AND EVENTS:
- *The Littlest World of Insects*
- *The Cry of the Sandhill Crane*
- *Migratory Bird Walk*
- *On the Trail of Whitetail Deer*
- *McHenry dam bird walk*
- *Fall colors*
- *Bird migration*
- *Lake Defiance bird walk*

DESCRIPTION: Filled with gravel-rich deposits that make up the park's wooded hills and ridges, Moraine Hills State Park in McHenry County offers 1,690 acres of geologic formations, including wetlands and lakes. A .5-mile loop boardwalk, with accompanying interpretive guide brochure, leads to a lake overlook. Also visible along the trail are various grasses, willows, waterfowl, and shorebirds. The interpretive guide highlights the aquatic life and wildlife that may be seen in the area.

REGULATIONS: Remain on trails. Do not remove anything. Pets must be leashed.

HOURS: The park closes at sundown.

DIRECTIONS: From US 12, go west on IL 176 for 3.75 miles to River Road, turn north, and go 2 miles to the entrance. Follow the main park road to the North Woods parking area or to the nature center building.

CONTACT INFORMATION: Moraine Hills State Park, Interpretive Programs, 914 S. River Rd., McHenry, IL 60050; (815) 385-1624; www.dnr.state.il.us/lands/landmgt/parks/r2/morhills.htm

7. Chain O' Lakes State Park

HIGHLIGHTS:
- *Accessible picnic area and trail*
- *4 trail systems*
- *2,793-acre park*
- *3 natural lakes (Grass, Marie, and Nippersink) and the Fox River*

DESCRIPTION: In the geographic center of Chain O' Lakes State Park in northwest Lake County lies the **Pike Marsh Trail** at the Pike Marsh North Picnic Area. The entire picnic area and trail were developed with disabled and elderly visitors in mind, offering comfortable access and views to all the natural wonders in the area. Along the trail are benches for rest stops and nature observation. The picnic area tables and rest rooms are well designed. The trail is a .5-mile loop and has a surface of crushed limestone. The best times to visit are late summer and fall.

REGULATIONS: Pets must be leashed.

HOURS: The park is open daily, 6:00 AM–9:00 PM, in summer; 8:00 AM to sunset, in winter.

DIRECTIONS: Take IL 173 west out of Antioch for 6 miles and turn south at Wilmot Road for 1.75 miles to the park entrance.

CONTACT INFORMATION: Chain O' Lakes State Park, 8916 Wilmot Rd., Spring Grove, IL 60081; (847) 587-5512; www.dnr.state.il.us/lands/landmgt/parks/r2/chaino.htm

8. Illinois Beach State Park

HIGHLIGHTS:
- *National Natural Landmark*
- *Hands-on exhibit area*
- *Outdoor education park staff*
- *Educational displays*
- *Viewing platform*
- *829-acre Illinois Nature Preserve*
- *Lake Michigan*
- *Wildflowers*
- *4,160-acre park*
- *Visitor center*
- *Multimedia presentations of the park's natural, historical, and recreational features*
- *Seasonal programs*

DESCRIPTION: Illinois Beach State Park is a captivating natural resource 10 miles south of the Illinois-Wisconsin state line in Lake County. The park has dramatic ridges and areas of dunes, marshes, and oak forests and a vast array of vegetation and animal life. The visitor center and nature trails are part of Illinois Beach State Park's southern unit, with 5 miles of connecting loop trails designed to show the tremendous diversity of the lakeshore. The trails also traverse an Illinois Nature Preserve. The nature preserve is comprised of 829 acres of diverse dune topography and features numerous plant species, including colorful wildflowers and many varieties of grasses and sedges as well as pines and deciduous trees. The trail itself is a sandy-soil surface, and the best times to visit are late spring, summer, and fall.

REGULATIONS: Pets must be leashed at all times.

HOURS: The park is open daily except Christmas.

DIRECTIONS: From US 41, take Wadsworth Road east across Sheridan Road (IL 137) to the park entrance.

CONTACT INFORMATION: Illinois Beach State Park, Zion, IL 60099; (847) 662-4811; www.dnr.state.il.us/lands/landmgt/parks/r2/ilbeach.htm

9.   Volo Bog State Natural Area

HIGHLIGHTS:
- *National Natural Landmark*
- *864-acre site*
- *161-acre Illinois Nature Preserve*
- *Only "quaking" bog in Illinois*
- *Visitor center with various exhibits, gift shop, and programs*
- *Prairie*
- *170 bird species*
- *Interpretive boardwalk trail*
- *The Bog Log newsletter*

PROGRAMS AND EVENTS:
- *Youth programs (e.g., Bog Life, Pond Life, Aqua Safari, Animal Homes, Birds, Mammals, Insect Safari, Animal Tracking, Small Wonders—A Sensory Walk, Nature Discovery, Animal Adaptations, Tomorrow's Leaders)*
- *Adult groups (e.g., Volo Bog: An Introduction to a Unique Illinois Wetland, Bog Botany, Pond Life, Tree and Shrub Identification, Bird Walk, Animal Tracking, Rediscovering the Wonder Within)*
- *Guided tours of Volo Bog*
- *Earthfest*
- *Lectures and workshops*
- *Bird walks*
- *Spring astronomy nights*
- *Signs of Spring hike*
- *Bog botany workshops*
- *Monthly reading group*

DESCRIPTION: Volo Bog is a unique natural area preserved by the State of Illinois 40 miles northwest of Chicago in Lake County. This 864-acre site consists of bogs, marshes, and restored prairies. A restored barn serves as a visitor center, providing information, exhibits, and a bookstore. A staff naturalist is available for tours of the bog. Two trails allow the visitor to explore the site. The **Tamarack View Trail** is a 2.75-mile hiking and cross-country skiing trail taking visitors through wetlands, woods, and prairie, with views of Volo Bog. The easier and much shorter **Volo Bog Interpretive Trail** is a .5-mile interpretive loop from the visitor center along a wood-chip path to a floating boardwalk in the bog.

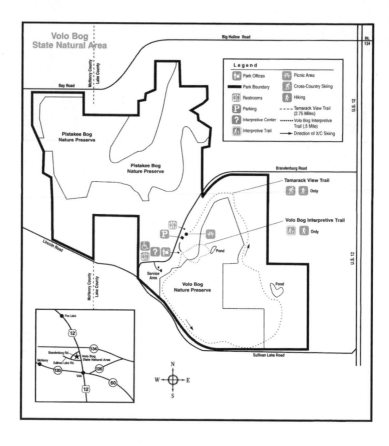

Numbered posts are along the trail, and seasonal guides describing the flora and fauna are available.

REGULATIONS: No bicyclists, horse riders, pets, food, smoking, or alcoholic beverages allowed. No plant or animal collecting permitted. Stay on trails.

HOURS: The site is open daily, 8:00 AM–4:00 PM. The visitor center is open Wednesday–Sunday, 9:00 AM–3:00 PM. Guided tours of the bog are on Saturday and Sunday.

DIRECTIONS: From US 12, go 1.5 miles north of IL 120, turn west on Sullivan Road, and proceed 1.9 miles to the entrance on the right side of the road.

CONTACT INFORMATION: Volo Bog State Natural Area, 28478 W. Brandenberg Rd., Ingleside, IL 60041; (815) 344-1294; www.dnr.state.il.us/lands/landmgt/parks/r2/volobog.htm

10. Ryerson Woods Forest Preserve

HIGHLIGHTS:
- *Woodlands*
- *Visitor center listed on the National Register of Historic Places*
- *Log cabins*
- *274-acre Illinois Nature Preserve*
- *Restored prairie*
- *Butterfly garden*
- *150 bird species*
- *500 species of flowering plants*
- *Farm area*
- *Wildflowers*
- *Floodplain forest*
- *6 miles of trails, including interpretive and accessible trails*

PROGRAMS AND EVENTS:
- *Teacher programs*
- *Guided and self-guided school and youth group programs*
- *Nature Explorers*
- *Wildflower Walks*
- *Sunday Bird Walks*
- *Plant Monitoring Workshop*
- *Knee-High Naturalists*
- *Planting projects*
- *Conservation work days*

DESCRIPTION: Ryerson Woods Forest Preserve is in a beautiful 550-acre woodland and floodplain forest adjoining the Des Plaines River in Lake County. Found at the site is a visitor center, cabins, a farm, and 6 miles of trails with views of wildflowers and forest. The visitor center, listed on the National Register of Historic Places, is a large mansion that was once the summer estate of the Edward L. Ryerson family, who donated the land to the forest preserve. A few interpretive and accessible trails are described here.

The **Ned Ryerson Trail** is a .25-mile accessible loop on packed gravel that begins at the parking area and goes by a butterfly garden and a prairie and through the forest for a short distance before it loops back to the parking area. Informational signs are seen along this trail, and it connects with other park trails. An audiotape about the area's nature is available from the visitor center for listening while on this trail.

Interpretive sign found along trail, Ryerson Woods Forest Preserve

The **South Wildflower Trail,** .5 mile in length, takes the visitor from the parking area south to the Des Plaines River and north through woodlands to the Exhibit Cabin. Numbered posts corresponding to one of the trail brochures describe the wildflowers and trees along the trail. Wildflowers that may be seen include mayapple, great white trillium, common violet, bloodroot, trout lily, and wild geranium.

The **North Trail** is a .4-mile loop that begins behind the Program Cabin and leads through a floodplain forest. Numbered posts along the dirt trail are described in the trail booklet. An overlook of the Des Plaines River and a boardwalk over a wetland are encountered at the start of the trail.

REGULATIONS: No collecting or picking of plants allowed. Stay on trails. Park in designated areas only. Bicycles allowed on paved roads only. Off-road vehicles, pets, fires, firearms, hunting, camping, swimming, and wading are prohibited.

HOURS: The preserve is open daily, 6:30 AM–5:00 PM; until sunset on Wednesdays in summer. The visitor center is open daily, 9:00 AM–5:00 PM, except Thanksgiving, Christmas, and New Year's Day. The cabins are open on Wednesday afternoons and weekends.

DIRECTIONS: From I-94, turn west on IL 22, travel 1 mile to Riverwoods Road, turn south, and travel 1.3 miles to the entrance on the west side of the road.

CONTACT INFORMATION: Ryerson Woods Forest Preserve, 21950 N. Riverwoods Rd., Deerfield, IL 60015; (847) 968-3321; www.ryersonwoods@co.lake.il.us/forest/educate.htm

11.   Heller Nature Center

HIGHLIGHTS:
- *Nature center with exhibits*
- *Staff naturalist*
- *Log cabin*
- *Restored prairies*
- *Pond with observation deck*
- *Accessible trails*
- *Classroom in the woods*

PROGRAMS AND EVENTS:
- *Nature Ranger*
- *Bird Feeding*
- *Beginning Bird-Watching*
- *Summer nature camps*
- *Maple syrup harvest*
- *Wildflower walks*
- *Family campfire circle*

DESCRIPTION: The Heller Nature Center and associated trail system is in Highland Park (Lake County). The site has 97 acres of woods, wildflowers, restored prairies, wetlands, and oak savanna; a visitor center; 4 compacted-rock and wood-chip loop trails totaling 2.25 miles in length (2 of them accessible); a classroom in the woods; a log cabin; and a pond with an observation deck. The trails are all interconnected and range from .3 mile to 1 mile in length; the accessible trails are .3 and .75 miles long. Found along the trail are trail boards as well as benches. The trails are color coded (green, yellow, blue, and red) and start outside the visitor center. They wind through some wooded stretches including an oak savanna, past some large cottonwoods, and into a stand of pine trees.

REGULATIONS: No bikes, horses, or motorized vehicles allowed on trails. Leash all pets. All plants and animals are protected. No alcoholic beverages or camping permitted. No releasing of wildlife allowed except by permit.

HOURS: The park is open daily, 6:00 AM to dusk. The visitor center is open Monday–Saturday, 8:30 AM–5:00 PM; Sunday, 10:00 AM–4:00 PM; closed July 4, Thanksgiving, Christmas, and New Year's Day.

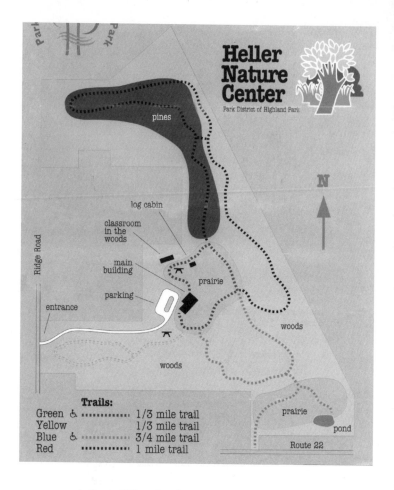

DIRECTIONS: From US 41, head west on IL 22 for 1.3 miles to Ridge Road, turn north and proceed .3 mile to the entrance on the east side of the road.

CONTACT INFORMATION: Heller Nature Center, 2821 Ridge Rd., Highland Park, IL 62249; (847) 433-6901; www.pdhp.org

12. Mississippi Palisades State Park

HIGHLIGHTS:
- *National Natural Landmark*
- *Views of the Mississippi River*
- *Developed overlooks*
- *Varied plants and wildlife*
- *Campgrounds*
- *Accessible trail*
- *48-acre Illinois Nature Preserve*

DESCRIPTION: Mississippi Palisades State Park, 3 miles north of Savanna in Carroll County, is a dedicated National Natural Landmark because of the many steep cliffs and outstanding vistas of the Mississippi River. **Oak Point Overlook** has an accessible path, 6 feet wide, .12 mile long, made of concrete and with handrails, leading to the overlook. The overlook and picnic tables are suitable for individuals with limited mobility. There are also 11 miles of hiking trails within the park.

REGULATIONS: Remain on trails. Do not remove anything.

HOURS: The park closes at sundown.

DIRECTIONS: From US 52, go north on IL 84 for 3 miles. The Oak Point Overlook is accessed from either the south or north park entrances.

CONTACT INFORMATION: Mississippi Palisades State Park, 4577 Route 84 North, Savanna, IL 61074; (815) 273-2731; www.dnr.state.il.us/lands/landmgt/parks/r1/palisade.htm

13. Jarrett Prairie Center

HIGHLIGHTS:
- *Staff naturalist*
- *Prairie grasses, including little bluestem, northern dropseed, side-oats grama, Indian grass*
- *Various wildflowers*
- *Gift shop*
- *300-acre prairie*
- *116-acre Illinois Nature Preserve*

PROGRAMS AND EVENTS:
- *Prairie Restoration Management*
- *Ranger Rick*
- *Nature classes*
- *Concerts*
- *Sky viewing*
- *Bird walks*
- *Prairie walks*
- *Outdoor education*

DESCRIPTION: The Jarrett Prairie Center on the southern edge of Byron in Ogle County is a modern facility that includes a natural history museum and gift shop. Classes and other functions are held in the center. There are 4 main trails totaling 2 miles in the preserve: **Loop Prairie Trail** near the north shelter, **Roundabout Trail** adjacent to the Jarrett Prairie Center, **Four Hills Trail,** and the **Indigo Trace Trail.** The trail surfaces are mowed grass and dirt. The shortest trail, the Roundabout, also connects to the longest loop trail, the Four Hills Trail, which has a separate spur at the west side going over to a scenic overlook. All along these trails and in the surrounding prairie there are goldenrod, flowering spurge, rough blazing star, and naked sunflower, which can be seen in full bloom during late summer.

REGULATIONS: No dogs allowed on interior hiking trails. Stay on trails.

HOURS: The nature center is open Monday–Saturday, 8:30 AM– 4:30 PM; Sunday, 1:00–4:30 PM.

DIRECTIONS: From the junction of IL 2 and IL 72 in Byron, follow IL 72 south across the Rock River to the park entrance off North River Road, just west of North German Church Road and the vehicle bridge over the Rock River.

CONTACT INFORMATION: Byron Forest Preserve District, 7993 N. River Rd., PO Box 1075, Byron, IL 61010-1075; (815) 234-8535

14. White Pines Forest State Park

HIGHLIGHTS:
- *Accessible trail*
- *Wildlife observation area*
- *Illinois Nature Preserve*
- *Cabins*

DESCRIPTION: In the heart of the Rock River Valley, 8 miles southwest of Oregon in Ogle County, this charming 385-acre park is the southern boundary of the former Chicago-Iowa Trail. In October 1997, a new .5-mile trail of crushed rock was developed to make the park more accessible to individuals with physical challenges. The trail begins at the parking lot on the east side of the White Pines Inn. This eastern border of the park is adjacent to a designated Illinois Nature Preserve. At the end of the trail is an accessible viewing stand. Additionally, there are 7 other hiking trails in the park.

REGULATIONS: Remain on trails. Do not remove anything.

HOURS: The park is open daily, sunrise to sunset.

DIRECTIONS: From the junction of IL 2 and IL 64 in Oregon, follow Pines Road southwest for 8 miles. The entrance is along the north side of the road, just past Pine Creek.

CONTACT INFORMATION: White Pines Forest State Park, 6712 W. Pines Rd., Mt. Morris, IL 61054; (815) 946-3717, TDD (217) 782-9175; www.dnr.state.il.us/lands/landmgt/parks/r2/whitepns.htm

15.   Castle Rock State Park

HIGHLIGHTS:

- *2,000-acre park*
- *685-acre Illinois Nature Preserve*
- *Wildlife viewing*
- *Sandstone outcroppings*
- *Hillside prairies*
- *Rock River valley*
- *Canoe camping area*
- *Hunting shelters*

DESCRIPTION: Land acquisition for Castle Rock State Park, south of Oregon in Ogle County, began in 1970. Currently, the park consists of 2,000 acres, 685 of which are an Illinois Nature Preserve—one of the largest significant natural areas in northern Illinois. Two self-guided nature trails, the **Heather Valley Trail** and the **Timber Edge Trail,** form short loops that total about 2 miles of mostly sandy soil surface. There are 28 numbered stations corresponding to descriptions in a trail brochure of the vast array of plant life, changing topography, and other natural features of the area. The brochure is available at the wildlife viewing trail sign, across the road from the Aspen Ridge Picnic Area. Shorter hikes are available on the 3 other trails in the north area and on the 3 trails in the south area of the park. The best time to visit is spring.

REGULATIONS: Pets must be leashed.

HOURS: The park is open daily except Christmas.

DIRECTIONS: From Oregon, go south on IL 2 for 3 miles to the entrance for the north area.

CONTACT INFORMATION: Castle Rock State Park, 1365 W. Castle Rd., Oregon, IL 61061; (815) 732-7329; www.dnr.state.il.us/lands/landmgt/parks/r1/castle.htm

16. Russell Woods Forest Preserve

HIGHLIGHTS:
- *Natural resource center*
- *Kishwaukee River*
- *Accessible campsites*
- *Accessible trail*

DESCRIPTION: The Russell Woods Forest Preserve is 1.75 miles southwest of Genoa, in DeKalb County. The natural resource center is home to many outdoor activities and programs. There are 3 trails within the preserve, and their surfaces vary from asphalt to dirt and mowed grass. The most accessible trail is a .12-mile-long, asphalt-paved loop around the north side of the natural resource center. Seen along this trail are various deciduous trees such as oaks. The **Upland Trail** is .3 mile long and meanders along the northern border of the preserve, mostly paralleling the campgrounds and the preserve road. The **Lowland Trail** offers the most scenic and challenging hike; however, during periods of high rainfall, it may become impassable. From the natural resource center and parking area, this trail begins by crossing the footbridge over the Kishwaukee River and then loops around about .5 mile through mostly deciduous forest.

REGULATIONS: Remain on trails. Do not remove anything.

HOURS: The preserve is open daily, sunrise to sunset.

DIRECTIONS: From Genoa, take IL 72 west for 1 mile to the preserve road on the left.

CONTACT INFORMATION: Red Oak Nature Center, 2343 S. River St., Batavia, IL 60510; (630) 897-1808

17.   Afton Forest Preserve

HIGHLIGHTS:
- *Self-guided nature trail*
- *Wildlife refuge*
- *Wetland*
- *Historic railroad bridge*

DESCRIPTION: The Afton Forest Preserve, a 240-acre wildlife and recreation area in the DeKalb County Forest Preserve District, offers the visitor exposure to a restored prairie, wetlands, and meadows. The self-guided nature trail winds along and through the wildlife refuge, completing a 1.25-mile loop—.75 mile on asphalt and .5 mile on mowed grass—displaying a diversity of plants and wildlife. The trail has 9 numbered stations with follow-along descriptions in the trail guide. Some common trees seen in the preserve are sugar maple and red oak, and some common prairie plants include the big bluestem, prairie dock, and goldenrod. Wildflower viewing is possible in the spring, summer, and fall. Common birds include kestrels, bobolink, killdeer, and great blue heron. Raccoon, skunk, and white-tailed deer are also common in the area. It is recommended that a guide be obtained from the county forest preserve office prior to visiting the preserve.

REGULATIONS: Stay on nature trail. Dogs must be leashed.

HOURS: The preserve is open daily, 8:00 AM to sunset.

DIRECTIONS: From I-88 (the East-West Tollway), exit east of DeKalb at Crego Road and go south 3.5 miles. From DeKalb, follow IL 23 south for 3.5 miles to Perry Road, go east 1 mile to Crego Road, and head south 1.25 miles to the entrance.

CONTACT INFORMATION: DeKalb County Forest Preserve District, 110 E. Sycamore St., Sycamore, IL 60178; (815) 895-7191, (815) 756-6633

18. Shabbona Lake State Park

HIGHLIGHTS:
- *1,550-acre park*
- *Accessible trails*
- *Restaurant*
- *Boat rental*

DESCRIPTION: Grass-covered meadows, upland mesic woods, bottom-land woods, a native marsh, and a 318-acre constructed lake are all part of the 1,550 acres within Shabbona Lake State Park in DeKalb County. The **Touch the Earth Trail** is an accessible trail at the north end of the Somonauk Point picnic and parking area. This .12-mile, one-way trail is 4 to 5 feet wide, made of crushed rock and compacted dirt, and offers a scenic lakeshore nature experience. An audiotape and trail brochure are available at the park office. Throughout the park are dedicated facilities designed for disabled visitor accessibility, including parking, picnic shelters, water fountains, rest rooms, telephones, and a fishing pier. There are 4.5 miles of additional hiking trails within the state park.

REGULATIONS: Remain on trails. Do not remove anything.

HOURS: The park is open daily, 6:00 AM–10 PM, in summer; 8:00 AM to sundown, in winter.

DIRECTIONS: From US 30 in Shabbona, follow Shabbona Road south to Preserve Road, turn east for .25 mile, and follow the sign to the park entrance.

CONTACT INFORMATION: Shabbona Lake State Park, 4201 Shabbona Grove Rd., Shabbona, IL 60550; (815) 824-2106, TDD (217) 782-9175; www.dnr.state.il.us/lands/landmgt/parks/r1/shabbona.htm

19. Tekakwitha Woods Nature Center

- *Arlene H. Shoemaker Nature Center*
- *Hands-on exhibits and displays*
- *Bird-feeding station*
- *Interpretive center*
- *Nature library*
- *Prairie restoration*
- *Historic McGuire House*
- The Tree Line *newsletter*

PROGRAMS AND EVENTS:

- *Scout programs*
- *School programs*
- *Plant identification*
- *Nature hikes*

DESCRIPTION: Tekakwitha Woods, a 65-acre parcel along the "big bend" of the Fox River in St. Charles (Kane County), was formerly owned by the Catholic Church. Tekakwitha was the name of the first Native American considered for canonization. There are 2 main trail sections at Tekakwitha Woods: north of the nature center building down to the Fox River, and west of the historic McGuire House. The **North Trail** parallels the Fox River; at the trail's eastern boundary, it connects with the Fox River Bike Trail. The western boundary of the north trail goes to the preserve boundary along Park Place Road. The **Western Loop Trail** winds southwest from the McGuire House and back to the parking lot. The trails at Tekakwitha pass through oak-hickory woodland and forested ravines, and they offer many views of native wildflowers and the Fox River as well as wildlife. The 1.5 miles of trails are mostly dirt and mowed grass.

REGULATIONS: Remain on trails. Do not remove anything. No pets, bicycles, or smoking allowed on trails.

HOURS: The trails are open daily, 8:00 AM to sunset. Nature center— April–November, open Monday–Thursday, 9:00 AM–4:00 PM; Saturday and Sunday, 12:00–4:00 PM; closed Friday. December–March, open Monday and Wednesday, 9:00 AM–4:00 PM; Tuesday and Thursday, by appointment; Saturday and Sunday, 1:00–4:00 PM; closed Friday.

DIRECTIONS: From St. Charles, take IL 25 north for 2.25 miles to Pinelands Road. Turn west (left) and go to Weber Drive. Turn north (right) and continue across Villa Marie Road to the parking lot.

CONTACT INFORMATION: Tekakwitha Woods, 35W076 Villa Marie Rd., St. Charles, IL 60174; (847) 741-8350

20. Peck Farm Park

HIGHLIGHTS:
- *Peck House and Nature Discovery Room with games and exhibits*
- *Observation silo*
- *Orientation barn with exhibits*
- *Restored prairie*
- *Wetlands and Peck Lake*
- *Gardens*
- *Accessible trails*
- *Wildflowers*

PROGRAMS AND EVENTS:
- *Classes (e.g., home landscaping, gardening, birding, ecology for adults, and nature exploration)*
- *School field trips*
- *Wildland Explorers Summer Nature and Hiking Adventure and Wilderness Survival Camps*

DESCRIPTION: Peck Farm Park, in Geneva (Kane County), is an old farmstead built in 1869 by Eli and Jerasha Peck and their children. The Peck family owned the farm until the early 1990s, when they donated the land to be preserved in its natural state. Today the farm, the Peck House and Nature Discovery Room, Peck Lake, the orientation barn and observation silo, the wetlands, a restored prairie, more than a mile of trails, and soccer and other ball fields are on this farm/park complex, which was formally dedicated in 1998. Trails lead from the barn and silo, formerly used to store grain. A set of stairs leads to the top of the silo for an excellent view of the complex. Wildflowers nearby provide some good photo opportunities. An accessible trail (rock surfaced) leads down the hillside towards Peck Lake and connects with a wood-chip trail that leads to the prairie and wetland complex. Other trails lead to the Geneva Middle School as well as around the ball fields.

REGULATIONS: Stay on trails.

HOURS: The picnic area and trails are open daily. The barn and silo are open Tuesday–Saturday, 8:00 AM–5:30 PM; Sunday, 12:00–4:00 PM. The Peck House is open Tuesday–Friday, 1:00–5:30 PM; Saturday, 10:00 AM–3:00 PM.

Prairie and orientation barn, Peck Farm Park

DIRECTIONS: In Geneva, take Randall Road to Fargo Road, 1.5 miles south of IL 38. Turn west and go .2 mile to Kaneville Road. Turn left and go 1 mile; the farm/park complex is on the left side of the road.

CONTACT INFORMATION: Peck Farm Park, Geneva Park District, 38W199 Kaneville Rd., Geneva, IL 60134; (630) 262-8244; www.genevaparks.org/links/peck.html

21.   Fermi National Accelerator Laboratory

HIGHLIGHTS:
- *Restored prairie and savanna*
- *Interpretive trail*
- *Oak woodlands*
- *Bison enclosure*

DESCRIPTION: Fermi National Accelerator Laboratory in Batavia (Kane County) is a US Department of Energy research facility consisting of various buildings and the 4-mile accelerator ring known as the Tevatron. Also found on the grounds at Fermi Lab is the **Prairie Interpretive Trail,** also referred to as the **Margaret Pearson Memorial Trail** in honor of her hard work and dedication to restore prairie habitat. The prairie has been restored since 1975 and is an excellent place to view native prairie plants. There is also a savanna. Two trail loops start from the parking area, a 1.5-mile outer loop and a .5-mile inner loop. Information signs describe the plants, the prairie, insects, the role of fires, and so on. The outer loop, being on the highest relief of the property, has a good view of the prairie and Fermi Lab. A bike trail also goes through the lab property.

REGULATIONS: Stay on paths. Do not litter. Yield to wildlife. No motorized vehicles allowed on trails. No collecting, picking flowers, camping, entry to restricted areas, firearms, fireworks, hunting, off-road vehicles, speeding, swimming in ponds, snowmobiles, trapping, or unaccompanied children are permitted. Keep all dogs leashed.

HOURS: Fermi Lab grounds are open daily, 6:00 AM–8:00 PM. Self-guided tours of Fermi Lab are available daily, 8:30 AM–5:00 PM.

DIRECTIONS: From I-88 (the East-West Tollway), take the Kirk Road exit. Go north for 8 miles to the entrance to Fermi Lab at Pine Street on the east side of the road. Turn east at Pine onto Fermi Lab grounds and travel .7 mile to a crossroad. Turn left and go 1 block to the parking area and trailhead.

CONTACT INFORMATION: Fermi National Accelerator Laboratory, PO Box 500, Batavia, IL 60510-0500; (630) 840-3351; www.fnal.gov

22. Waubansee Community College Nature Trail

HIGHLIGHTS:
- *Interpretive trail*
- *Wildflowers*

DESCRIPTION: The **Waubansee Community College Nature Trail** in Sugar Grove (Kane County) was originally proposed in 1975 as part of a refuge that would include the development of a wildflower area and a permanent nature trail around the college campus and designated wild areas. Today, the trail is a 2-mile, self-guided loop that begins on the south side of the building A parking lot. There are 28 interpretive signs along the trail to explain the features, which include Blackberry Creek, a swampland, and a grove of oak trees. Most of the trail surface is mowed grass and compacted dirt. Two excellent brochures about the nature trail are available from the public relations department at Waubansee Community College, *Nature Trail: Your Guide* and *Nature Trail: A Guide to Wildflowers*.

REGULATIONS: Remain on trails. Do not remove anything.

HOURS: The trail is open daily, sunrise to sunset.

DIRECTIONS: From I-88 (the East-West Tollway), take the US 30/ IL 47-Sugar Grove exit and head south on IL 56 to Galena Boulevard. Turn right (west) and proceed to IL 47. Turn right (north) and go 2 miles to the college.

CONTACT INFORMATION: Waubansee Community College, Sugar Grove Campus, Route 47 at Harter Rd., Sugar Grove, IL 60554-9799; (630) 466-7900, ext. 2411

23. Red Oak Nature Center

HIGHLIGHTS:
- *Nature center*
- *Fox River*
- *Observation deck*
- *Devil's Cave and associated interpretive boardwalk*
- *40-acre oak and maple forest*
- *Museum with interactive exhibits*
- *Plant and insect observation room*
- *Live animals on display*
- *Staff naturalist*

PROGRAMS AND EVENTS:
- *Nature programs*
- *Seasonal highlights in the multipurpose room*
- *Group tours*

DESCRIPTION: Red Oak Nature Center is within a 40-acre oak and maple forest, on the east banks of the Fox River in Kane County. Inside the nature center building, visitors will find a museum featuring interactive exhibits. The **Dolomite Trail** is about .5 mile long and is accessed directly behind (on the north side) of the nature center and at the observation deck. There are interpretive signs along the trail. The **Big Turtle Trail,** the most popular trail for families with small children, is a .25-mile loop accessed from the south and west side of the nature center and observation deck. A hike southward down the paved **Fox River Trail** leads to Devil's Cave natural ravine area and boardwalk. Another .12 mile or so south of Devil's Cave is the **Big Woods Trail,** a 1.5-mile loop when combined with the paved Fox River Trail. Also, about .25 mile north of the nature center and accessed from the Fox River Trail is the **Red Fox Prairie Trail.** Prairie grasses, large bur oaks, and a freshwater spring may be seen along this .5-mile loop. Some sections of trails within the Red Oak Nature Center system are in low-lying areas and may be challenging during periods of heavy rainfall—check with staff personnel for trail conditions before hiking.

REGULATIONS: Remain on trails. Do not remove anything.

HOURS: The site is open weekdays, 9:00 AM–4:30 PM; weekends, 10:00 AM–3:00 PM.

DIRECTIONS: From Aurora, follow IL 25 north on the east side of the Fox River about .5 mile past the IL 56 junction and watch for the sign to the center and parking lot on the left.

CONTACT INFORMATION: Red Oak Nature Center, 2343 S. River St., Batavia, IL 60510; (630) 897-1808

24. Chicago Botanic Garden

HIGHLIGHTS:
- *385-acre botanic garden and natural area*
- *15 acres of restored prairies*
- *20 garden areas*
- *Over 1.5 million plants*
- *Native flora of Illinois*
- *Education center*
- *Over 250 bird species*

PROGRAMS AND EVENTS:
- *School programs*
- *Gardening programs*
- *Midwest Gardening Certificate Program*
- *Ornamental Plant Materials Certificate Program*
- *Landscape Design courses*
- *Natural Studies (e.g., woodland wildflower walks, bird walks, prairie walks, bird-watching for people with mobility impairments)*
- *Spring Blooms Walks*
- *Grand Tram Tours*
- *Botanical arts courses*
- *Earth Day concert*
- *Spring concert*
- *Spring plant sale*
- *Plant society shows*
- *Summer gardening festival*
- *Fall shows*

DESCRIPTION: The Chicago Botanic Garden is a beautiful, 385-acre facility in Glencoe and owned by the Forest Preserve District of Cook County. The 23 landscaped gardens are home to over 1.5 million plants. Restored prairies, the Skokie Lagoon ponds, and the 100-acre McDonald Woods are here, as well as an education center, garden shop, gift shop, and conference rooms. Visitors may stroll around the garden areas on paved paths or hike a nature trail through the McDonald Woods. The nature trail (dirt and wood-chip surfaced) follows a wooded tract with numerous ferns and wildflowers. There is an entrance fee to the Chicago Botanic Garden.

Tulips and swans along a garden path, Chicago Botanic Garden

REGULATIONS: No climbing on trees and shrubs, picking fruits or vegetables, walking in garden beds, or collecting of plants, flowers, or shrubs permitted. No pets (except support animals), active sports and games, or alcohol allowed. Bikes permitted only on designated bike trails. Picnicking allowed in designated area only.

HOURS: The garden is open daily, 8:00 AM to sunset, except Christmas.

DIRECTIONS: From I-94, take IL 41 north 1 mile to Lake Cook Road. Head east for .7 mile to the entrance on the south side of the road.

CONTACT INFORMATION: Chicago Botanic Garden, 1000 Lake Cook Rd., Glencoe, IL 60022; (847) 835-5440, TDD (847) 835-0790; www.chicago-botanic.org

25. Crabtree Nature Center

HIGHLIGHTS:
- *Visitor center with numerous exhibits and programs*
- *1,100-acre complex*
- *Nature and interpretive trails*
- *Bird-watching area*
- *Restored prairie*
- *Marsh/wetlands*
- *265 bird species*

PROGRAMS AND EVENTS:
- *Ponds and Wetlands*
- *Nature of Spring*
- *Earth Day*
- *Nature walks*
- *Wildflower identification*
- *Bird day*
- *Pond life*

DESCRIPTION: Crabtree Nature Center is operated by the Forest Preserve District of Cook County. The site consists of 1,100 acres of marsh/wetlands and restored prairie, where numerous bird species may be seen. A visitor center provides information, exhibits (animals, plants, archaeology, prairies, weather), a book shop, and various programs for the public. Over 3 miles of trails wind through the grounds on a grass and dirt surface. The .3-mile **Giant's Hollow Trail** loops past Sulky Pond and Crabtree Lake, where there is a wildlife viewing platform. The **Bur Edge Trail** leads north from the visitor center on a 1.3-mile interpretive loop. The trail has lettered posts along the trail corresponding to descriptions in the trail booklet, and there are benches along the way. The **Phathom Trail** loops for 1.3 miles through a restored prairie and is reached from the Bur Edge Trail, north of the visitor center. At times, the trails may be extremely wet or inundated.

REGULATIONS: Pets, radios, musical instruments, picnics, food, and beverages are prohibited. Stay on trails. No littering or removal of plants or other natural objects allowed.

HOURS: The site is open weekdays, 8:00 AM–5:00 PM; weekends, 8:00 AM–5:30 PM, March–October, and 8:00 AM–4:30 PM, November–February. The visitor center is open weekdays, 9:00 AM–4:30 PM; weekends, 9:00 AM–5:00 PM, in summer, and 9:00 AM–4:00 PM, in winter.

DIRECTIONS: From I-90 in northwest Cook County, turn north on Barrington Road to Palatine Road. Turn west (left) and go about 1.5 miles to the entrance on the north side of the road.

CONTACT INFORMATION: Forest Preserve District of Cook County, 536 N. Harlem Ave., River Forest, IL 60305; (847) 381-6592

26.   River Trail Nature Center

HIGHLIGHTS:

- *Nature museum with gifts, books, exhibits (fish, snakes, mammals, Native Americans), and live animals (owl, hawk, fox)*
- *Restored prairie*
- *Des Plaines River floodplain forest*

PROGRAMS AND EVENTS:

- *Children's programs (e.g., Tales and Trails, Discovery Days, Small Serendipity)*
- *Evening programs (e.g., Evening Walks, Fireside Tales, Owls)*
- *Sunday and holiday special programs*
- *In-school programs*
- *Junior Naturalists*
- *Spring Wildflowers*
- *Fall Harvest and Honey Festival*
- *Earth Day*
- *Maple Syrup Festival*
- *Bird walks*

DESCRIPTION: River Trail Nature Center in Northbrook is operated by the Forest Preserve District of Cook County, along the Des Plaines River floodplain in the Allison Woods Forest Preserve holdings. The Potawatomi Indians once occupied the area, using the river as a transportation source. Maples and cottonwoods dominate the landscape, and wildflowers are found along the forest floor. The nature center has numerous exhibits on the local flora and fauna and on Native Americans. Outside the nature center building, live animals are kept in a half-dozen cages. Two connected dirt trails wind their way through the forest. The **Grove Portage Trail** is southeast of the nature museum and is .5 mile in length. It goes past the caged animals and then loops through the floodplain forest. The **Green Bay Trail,** .75 mile in length, begins outside the nature museum and heads north along the Des Plaines River and into the floodplain forest. It crosses a few small creeks, and a loop spur leads to the Allison Woods Picnic Site.

REGULATIONS: No pets, picnicking, horses, bicycles, radios, or loud noise allowed. All natural items are protected. Fishing allowed only at the Fishing Hole. Stay on trails.

HOURS: The grounds and trails are open daily, 8:00 AM–5:00 PM. The museum is open Monday–Thursday, 9:00 AM–4:30 PM; Saturday and Sunday, 9:00 AM–5:00 PM; closed on Friday.

DIRECTIONS: From I-294, head west on Willow Road for 1.25 miles to Milwaukee Avenue. Turn south and continue 1 mile to the entrance on the west side of the road.

CONTACT INFORMATION: River Trail Nature Center, 3120 N. Milwaukee Ave., Northbrook, IL 60062; (847) 824-8360; TDD (708) 771-1190

27. The Grove

HIGHLIGHTS:
- *Nature preserve*
- *Exhibits*
- *National Historic Landmark*
- *Wetlands*
- *Interpretive center*
- *Historic one-room schoolhouse*

PROGRAMS AND EVENTS:
- *School programs*
- *Fall Fest and Pumpkin Trail*
- *Nature Walk*
- *Grove Heritage Days*
- *Garden and antique show*

DESCRIPTION: The nature preserve and public museum in Glenview (Cook County) known as the Grove incorporates 123 acres of ecologically diverse land, including prairie, wetlands, and oak woodlands as well as many varieties of plants and wildlife. The self-guided wetland walkway is a .25-mile loop close to the interpretive center, where visitors may pick up a brochure that identifies 16 points of flora, fauna, and topography of the area. Duckweed, blue flag iris, and other plants may be seen along the walkway. There are 2 additional connecting loop trails. The interpretive center has many live fish and wildlife displays, and staff members are available for information and assistance.

REGULATIONS: Remain on trails. Do not remove anything. No smoking, fishing, pets, or bikes permitted on trails.

HOURS: The site is open Monday–Friday, 8:00 AM–4:30 PM (until 6:00 PM in summer); weekends, 9:00 AM–5:00 PM.

DIRECTIONS: The Grove is about 10 miles northwest of Chicago off of Milwaukee Avenue, .25 mile south of Lake Avenue. The entrance is on the east side of Milwaukee, just south of the I-294 overpass.

CONTACT INFORMATION: The Grove, 1421 Milwaukee Ave., Glenview, IL 60025; (847) 299-6096

28. Stephen R. Keay Nature Learning Center

HIGHLIGHTS:
- *Interpretive and accessible trail*
- *Waterfall*
- *Pond and viewing area*
- *Wildflowers*
- *Photo blind*

DESCRIPTION: The Stephen R. Keay Nature Learning Center is a small park in Wilmette (Cook County), named in honor of the director of the Northern Suburban Special Recreation Association. The 4.6-acre site has a .5-mile interpretive loop trail that winds through the property. The accessible trail is a hard-packed rock surface and has 28 numbered posts and an associated trail booklet describing the flora and fauna. The trail takes the visitor over a small pond, past a waterfall, and through a small wooded area. Found along the trail are benches, viewing areas, a photo blind overlooking the pond, water fountains, and tree identification markers.

REGULATIONS: Stay on trail surfaces. Do not remove any items from the park. Fishing or wading in the pond is prohibited. No dogs, alcoholic beverages, or open fires allowed.

HOURS: The park is open daily, April–September, 8:00 AM–7:00 PM; October–March, 8:00 AM–4:00 PM.

DIRECTIONS: From I-94, go east on Lake Avenue (exit 34) for 6 blocks to Skokie Boulevard. Turn south and travel for 2 blocks until it joins Hibbard Road. The entrance is off Hibbard Road on the east side.

CONTACT INFORMATION: Wilmette Park District, 1200 Wilmette Ave., Wilmette, IL 60091; (312) 256-6100

29. Schaumburg Township–District 54 Nature Center

HIGHLIGHTS:
- *12 wooded acres*
- *Seasonal marsh*
- *Restored prairie*
- *Environmental education trainers*
- *Hands-on education center*

PROGRAMS AND EVENTS:
- *Seasonal Changes*
- *Rocks to Soil*
- *Prairie Unit*
- *Science curriculum for grades K–5*

DESCRIPTION: The Schaumburg Township–District 54 Nature Center is behind the Frost Junior High School in Schaumburg (Cook County), 6 miles west of Chicago-O'Hare Airport. Just beyond the parking area and gated entrance is a visitor center that houses the classroom area, some exhibits, and the educational materials used by the nature center staff and the Schaumburg Township School District. An excellent short nature hike with an accompanying trail guide was designed primarily for use with the science curriculum for kindergarten, second grade, and fifth grade; however, the center is open to the public. There are 14 marked stations along the dirt and mowed grass paths. Directly behind the nature center, the trail borders marshland and passes through wooded areas. Continuing east past the boardwalk, the trail leads to an open marsh and an observation blind. The **Broken Windmill Trail** is the last loop before returning to the nature center. The total length is .5 mile.

REGULATIONS: Collecting or picking of flowers, plants, or anything found at the nature center is prohibited.

HOURS: Changes seasonally; call ahead.

DIRECTIONS: From I-90 in northwest Cook County, take Roselle Road south, turn west on Wise Road, and go 1 mile to Frost Junior High School; or take Barrington Road south and go east on Wise Road about 2 miles. Once inside the school parking lot, go around the east side of the building to the small parking area on the north side.

CONTACT INFORMATION: District 54 Nature Center, 320 W. Wise Rd., Schaumburg, IL 60193-4097; (847) 885-5816

30.   Spring Valley Nature Sanctuary and Volkening Heritage Farm

HIGHLIGHTS:

- *Nature center with various displays, hands-on exhibits, bookstore, library, and greenhouse*
- *135 acres of woods, wetlands, and trails*
- *Volkening Heritage Farm*
- *Observation silo*
- *Restored prairie*
- Natural Enquirer *newsletter*
- *Log cabin*
- *Wildflower gardens*
- *Illinois Heritage Grove Arboretum*
- *Accessible and interpretive trails*
- *Bob Link Arboretum*

PROGRAMS AND EVENTS:

- *School programs at Volkening Heritage Farm*
- *Jewels of the Prairie*
- *Eyes to the Sky*
- *Spring sugar bush fair*
- *Sundays at the cabin foodways and craft program*
- *Autumn pioneer festival*
- *Halloween ghost jaunt*
- *Old-fashioned Christmas*
- *Naturalist-guided tours*
- *Indoor and outdoor nature study and historic interpretation*

DESCRIPTION: Spring Valley Nature Sanctuary and Volkening Heritage Farm in Cook County is a park/farm complex operated by the Schaumburg Park District. The 135-acre site offers the visitor a chance to step back in time and see a restored prairie, wildflower garden, wetlands, arboretum, and an 1850s farmstead. Interpretive trails lead through the grounds, and connecting trails take the visitor to the Volkening Farm area and the Bob Link Arboretum. The visitor center has numerous hands-on exhibits and displays, a library, a greenhouse, and an observation silo, where stairs lead to a platform with a bird's-eye view of the property. Just west of the visitor center's parking area is a short trail to the wildflower garden. Other paths lead through the Volkening Farm, which has farm animals, a barn, a visitor center, a 150-year-old farmhouse, and various sheds and small buildings.

40

The **Illinois Habitat Trail** leads the visitor for 1.2 miles through the

1850s farm-stead, Spring Valley Nature Sanctuary and Volkening Heritage Farm

heart of the grounds, past restored prairies, wetlands, and ponds to a log cabin, the Volkening Farm, and the Bob Link Arboretum. The trail is partly accessible, with a paved portion that leads through the prairies and then north to the log cabin. The trail has 8 numbered posts corresponding to brief descriptions in the trail map brochure. A paved section of this trail also leads to the Illinois Heritage Grove (post 7), where trail signs identify the trees. In the southwest portion of the park is the 1-mile **Bob Link Trail,** which offers more seclusion among woods, wildflowers, and prairie.

REGULATIONS: No pets, bicycles, food, alcohol, radios, campfires, or roller blades allowed. No picnicking, fishing, skiing, snowmobiling, or jogging permitted. Stay on marked trails. No collecting of plants, animals, insects, fruits, seeds, stones, or other natural features allowed.

HOURS: The park grounds are open daily, 9:00 AM–5:00 PM, November–March; 9:00 AM–8:00 PM, April–October. The visitor center is open daily, 9:00 AM–5:00 PM. The Volkening Heritage Farm is open Thursday–Monday, 9:00 AM–5:00 PM, April–October.

DIRECTIONS: From I-290, head west on Higgins Road (exit 1B) for .8 mile to Meacham Road. Turn south and travel .8 mile to Schaumburg Road. Turn west and go .3 mile to the parking area for the nature center. To reach the Volkening Heritage Farm, continue on Schaumburg Road for .5 mile to Plum Grove Road. Turn south and go .4 mile to the parking area on the east side of the road.

CONTACT INFORMATION: Spring Valley Nature Sanctuary, 111 E. Schaumburg Rd., Schaumburg, IL 60194; (847) 985-2100; www.parkfun.com/spgvlly.html

31.   Wildwood Nature Center

HIGHLIGHTS:
- *Accessible trail and fishing pier*
- *Hands-on nature center with various exhibits and animals*
- *Prairie and garden*
- *Wildlife pond with observation deck*

PROGRAMS AND EVENTS:
- *Tree, insect, bird, hands-on animals, papermaking, animal tracking, and pond programs*
- *Earth Explorers*
- *Knapsackers*
- *Winter Wild*
- *Nature Friends*
- *Family Fun Days*
- *Scout programs and badge*
- *Teacher outreach program*
- *Campfire*
- *Camps (e.g., winter camp, before-and-after-care for winter camp, spring break camp, before-and-after-care for spring break camp, sports break camp)*

DESCRIPTION: Wildwood Nature Center is a small facility in Cook County within the 10-acre Maine Park owned by the City of Park Ridge. The nature center has many hands-on activities, exhibits, animals, and programs for the general public, plus a small pond, a fishing pier, and a .25-mile accessible trail (paved and gravel surfaced). Along the trail are a shelter, an observation deck, and benches. The pond is a great place to observe the birds nesting in the area or those migrating.

REGULATIONS: No swimming or skating allowed. No dogs permitted in park. Do not feed the birds.

HOURS: The nature center is open Monday–Friday, 3:30–6:30 PM; Saturday, 10:00 AM–2:00 PM; closed on Saturdays in winter. The park closes at dark.

DIRECTIONS: From I-294, head east on Touhy Avenue for 1 mile to Dee Road. Turn north and go .5 mile to Sibley Avenue. Turn west and continue for 5 blocks to Forestview. Turn south and proceed 5 blocks to the parking area.

CONTACT INFORMATION: Park Ridge Recreation and Park District, 2701 Sibley Ave., Park Ridge, IL 60068; (847) 692-3570; www.park-ridge.il.us/prpark/natctr.html

32. Emily Oaks Nature Center

- *Nature center with Discovery Room*
- *Nature and accessible trails*
- The Listening Post *newsletter*
- *Native grasses and wildflowers*
- *Pond*
- *Oak savanna*
- *Numerous bird species*

PROGRAMS AND EVENTS:

- *Tot programs (e.g., Young Explorers, Discovery Den, Fireside Storytime)*
- *Children's programs (e.g., Animal Edibles, Winter Game of Life, Build a Birdfeeder, Snow Print Detectives)*
- *Teen programs*
- *Adult programs (e.g., Butterflies in the Garden, Backyard Bird Feeding)*
- *Summer camp programs*
- *Youth group and Scout nature programs*
- *Things That Go Bump in the Night*
- *Tapestry of Lights*
- *Earth Day celebration*
- *Spring Equinox Chili Fest*
- *Pancake Breakfast in the Woods*
- *Autumn picnics*
- *Evening campfires*
- *Self-guided activities (e.g., trail kit, winter snowshoeing, woodland bingo)*

DESCRIPTION: Emily Oaks Nature Center is a 13-acre wooded tract and nature center in Skokie (Cook County) that features an outdoor education center built to allow individuals to interact with the natural environment. The site includes a nature center that offers various programs throughout the year; a paved, .25-mile, accessible trail; and another .3-mile, wood-chip and dirt path leading around a 3-acre pond. The paved trail loops through the middle of the site past a small wooded area, while the wood-chip trail leads around a pond where there are some great birding opportunities.

REGULATIONS: No fishing, biking, boating, pets, alcohol, fires, use of RV vehicles, picnicking, camping, competitive sports, or swimming permitted.

HOURS: The grounds are open daily until sunset. The nature center is open Monday–Friday, 8:00 AM–5:00 PM; Saturday, 8:00 AM–4:00 PM; and Sunday, 10:00 AM–4:00 PM.

DIRECTIONS: From I-94, head east on Touhy Avenue (exit 39B) for 6 blocks to Kostner Avenue. Turn north and go 6 blocks to Brummel Street. Turn west and go .5 mile to the entrance on the north side of the street.

CONTACT INFORMATION: Emily Oaks Nature Center, 4650 Brummel St., Skokie, IL 60076; (847) 677-7001

33.   Robinson Family Burial Grounds

HIGHLIGHTS:
> • *Burial grounds of Chief Alexander Robinson*
> *(Chief Chee-Chee-Pin-Quay) and family*
> • *Part of Indian Boundary Forest Division*
> *(Forest Preserve District of Cook County)*
> • *Accessible trail*

DESCRIPTION: The Robinson Family Burial Grounds in Chicago is part of the Forest Preserve District of Cook County, Robinson Woods North. A 250-foot paved trail takes the visitor to a granite rock inscribed with the account of Alexander Robinson (Chief Chee-Chee-Pin-Quay) and his wife, Catherine Chevalier. Robinson died in 1872, and according to the Treaty of Prairie Du Chien of 1827, he was to be buried on these grounds as the chief of the Potawatomi, Ottawa, and Chippewa nations. Near the granite rock are a pair of benches. Dirt paths lead towards the Des Plaines River and the Des Plaines River Trail.

REGULATIONS: Stay on trail.

HOURS: The site is open only during daylight for safety.

DIRECTIONS: From I-90, turn south on Cumberland Avenue and go 1.2 miles to Lawrence Avenue. Turn west and go .6 mile to East River Road. Turn north and go 1 block; parking is on the west side of the road.

CONTACT INFORMATION: Forest Preserve District of Cook County, Cummings Square, 536 N. Harlem Ave., River Forest, IL 60305; (773) 261-8400

34. North Park Village Nature Center

HIGHLIGHTS:
- *Nature center with various hands-on exhibits*
- *Children's room with books*
- *Stuffed animals*
- *Woodland prairie*
- *Restored wetlands*
- *Wildflowers*
- Urban Naturalist *newsletter*

PROGRAMS AND EVENTS:
- *All about Turtles*
- *Pond Prowl*
- *Turtle Show and Tell*
- *Animals in Winter*
- *All about Bats*
- *Terrific Trees*
- *Getting Ready for Winter*
- *Owl Prowl*
- *Family fun days*
- *Family nature walks*
- *Neighborhood Naturalist outreach*
- *Field trips (e.g., Maple tree tapping, wetlands, Native American culture walk, nature in water, nature discovery walk)*
- *Summer camp for eco-explorers*
- *Harvest festival*
- *Water solstice celebration*
- *Star watches*
- *Winter Solstice festival*
- *Native American activity time*
- *Bird feeders*
- *Migratory bird walks*
- *Composting workshops*
- *Story circle*
- *Fall plant identification*
- *Seed collection workshop*
- *Winter tree identification*
- *Teacher enhancement programs*

Hands-on exploring, North Park Village Nature Center

DESCRIPTION: The North Park Village Nature Center is on the North Side of Chicago. The 155-acre complex was formerly a tuberculosis sanatorium. In the early 1970s, the sanatorium was closed and the complex converted to other uses, including 46 acres that were dedicated as a nature preserve and nature center. Today this unique facility is within easy reach of 3,000,000 people. In addition to the nature center, the site features nature trails, a restored wetland and prairie, and an oak savanna woodland. Four main loop trails (1.5 miles in length) wind through the nature preserve. Numerous programs for children and adults are offered at the nature center.

REGULATIONS: Stay on trails. No smoking, feeding wildlife, collecting plants, hunting, trapping, fishing, skiing, sledding, or ice skating permitted. No pets or bikes allowed.

HOURS: The site is open daily, 10:00 AM–4:00 PM; closed Thanksgiving, Christmas, and New Year's Day.

DIRECTIONS: From I-90/94, go north on Pulaski Road (exit 44B). Two blocks north of Bryn Mawr Avenue, turn east at Ardmore Avenue and go 3 blocks, following the signs to the parking area.

CONTACT INFORMATION: North Park Village Nature Center, 5801 N. Pulaski Rd., Chicago, IL 60646; (312) 744-5472; TTY (312) 744-3586; www.ci.chi.il.us./env/NaturalResources/NorthParkVillage.html

35.   Brookfield Zoo

HIGHLIGHTS:
- *2,700 animals in zoo*
- *Children's zoo and dolphin presentation*
- *Salt Creek Wilderness*
- *Interpretive trail*
- *Indian Lake*
- *Dragonfly Marsh*
- *Motor safari*

DESCRIPTION: The Brookfield Zoo, on the outskirts of Chicago, is world-renowned for its exhibits, exotic animals, and beautifully landscaped grounds. At the west end of the zoo lies the Salt Creek Wilderness. Built in cooperation with the US Fish and Wildlife Service, this 10-acre exhibit features a nature trail paralleling Indian Lake and Salt Creek. The **Indian Lake Trail** is .25 mile in length and the surface is wood chip. There are various interpretive signs about wetlands, plants, and so on, plus a few overlooks of Indian Lake, and at the end of the trail is the Dragonfly Marsh Area, where an observation platform and a restored wetland are located. Brookfield Zoo also has various special events throughout the year, including Groundhog Day, Valentine's Day Celebration, National Pig Day, Spring Lecture Series, Arbor Day, International Migratory Bird Weekend, and a Rhythm and Roots Festival. Stroller, wheelchair, wagon, and electronic vehicle rentals are available. A parking and general admission fee are charged.

REGULATIONS: All buildings at the zoo are smoke free. Do not feed or chase animals or damage plants, and respect safety barriers. Bicycles and skates prohibited inside the zoo.

HOURS: The Indian Lake Trail and all buildings close 30 minutes before the zoo closes. The zoo is open January 1–April 1, daily, 10:00 AM–5:00 PM; April 2–May 26, weekdays, 10:00 AM–5:00 PM, and weekends, 10:00 AM–6:00 PM; May 27–December 31, daily, 9:30 AM–6:00 PM.

DIRECTIONS: From I-290, exit at 1st Avenue. Turn south and travel 3 miles, following the signs to Brookfield Zoo parking. From I-294 (the Tri-State Tollway), exit at Ogden Avenue and head east for 4.5 miles to

Salt Creek Wilderness trailhead, Brookfield Zoo

1st Avenue. Turn north and follow the signs 2 miles to the zoo. From I-55, exit at 1st Avenue (exit 282) and travel about 3 miles north to the parking area.

CONTACT INFORMATION: Brookfield Zoo, 3300 Golf Rd., Brookfield, IL 60513; (708) 485-0263; www.brookfieldzoo.org

36. Peggy Notebaert Nature Museum

HIGHLIGHTS:
- *Nature museum with various interpretive displays, hands-on exhibits, water lab, auditorium, and shop*
- *Judy Istock Butterfly Haven*
- *Children's gallery*
- *Wilderness walk*
- *Wildflower garden, native grass and butterfly garden*
- *Pond observation area*

PROGRAMS AND EVENTS:
- *Early childhood programs*
- *Self-guided programs*
- *Summer camps*
- *School workshops*
- *Adult education*
- *Educator retreats*
- *Science for youth (e.g., The Case of the Animals vs. Habitats, Microbe Towers)*
- *Science for families (e.g., Cool Collections, Build a Birdfeeder, Batty for Bats, Trees for Tots)*

DESCRIPTION: The Peggy Notebaert Nature Museum is the newest museum operated by the Chicago Academy of Sciences, on Chicago's Near North Side in Lincoln Park. The museum is a beautiful nature and science center offering many programs, hands-on activities, and displays including a family water lab, Environmental Central (a computer activity center), a children's gallery with a prairie home, a walk-in beaver lodge and fishing display, a city science area, a wilderness walk, and—the major highlight of the museum—the Judy Istock Butterfly Haven, where visitors stroll among 800 different species of butterflies in a greenhouse. Cocoons are raised in the greenhouse, and visitors can watch as butterflies emerge to take flight, and there are butterfly displays as well as a butterfly light show. Outside the museum, visitors can visit a wildflower garden, a successional garden, a native grass and butterfly garden, and a pond overlook. Bike trails link with the Lakefront Bike Path, and Lincoln Park Zoo is directly south of the museum. There is an entrance fee to the museum.

Reviewing an exhibit on butterflies, Peggy Notebaert Nature Museum

REGULATIONS: Stay on trails.

HOURS: The museum is open daily, 10:00 AM–5:00 PM, Labor Day to Memorial Day, and 10:00 AM–6:00 PM, Memorial Day to Labor Day; and every Wednesday until 8:00 PM. Closed on Thanksgiving, Christmas, and New Year's Day.

DIRECTIONS: From US 41 (Lake Shore Drive), take the Fullerton Avenue exit. Head west to Cannon Drive, turn north, and park along the drive. Parking is also available at the zoo.

CONTACT INFORMATION: Peggy Notebaert Nature Museum, 2430 N. Cannon Dr., Chicago, IL 60657; (773) 755-5100; 24-hour hotline (773) 871-2668; www.chias.org

37.   Chicago Portage National Historic Site

HIGHLIGHTS:
- *Historic land/water route linking the Great Lakes with the Mississippi River*
- *Site listed on the National Register of Historic Places*
- *Illinois and Michigan Canal National Heritage Corridor*
- *Sculpture of Marquette, Jolliet, and Native American*
- *Interpretive sign*
- *Portage Creek (old Des Plaines River channel)*
- *Site of Portage Trail*
- *Birding opportunities*

DESCRIPTION: No book on Illinois interpretive trails would be complete without a description of the historic Chicago Portage, on the continental divide between the Mississippi River drainage and Great Lakes drainage. This was the home of the land/water route between the Des Plaines River, a shallow body of water referred to as Mud Lake, and the south branch of the Chicago River, linking the Mississippi River to the Great Lakes. Native American land trails merging near this location led north to Green Bay, Wisconsin, west along the Illinois River, and to other Midwest locations. The land/water trail was used by Native Americans and French fur traders as well as by early pioneers and settlers to the area. Louis Jolliet and Father Jacques Marquette (the first Europeans to use the portage) and others knew of and traveled the Chicago Portage. This early transportation route led to the building of the Illinois and Michigan Canal (1848), which was an impetus for the rise of Chicago and made the portage trail obsolete. As a result of new transportation sources and the growth of Chicago, Mud Lake was filled in, and homes, commercial buildings, and factories were built, paving the way for the rise of the nation's third largest city.

Today, the Chicago Portage National Historic Site is preserved as a component of the Forest Preserve District of Cook County as the Chicago Portage Woods. Visitors can see the sculpture of Marquette and Jolliet and a Native American and walk the grass path down to the reconfigured Portage Creek. An interpretive sign may be seen to the left of the sculpture. A footpath loops around the site, and a few informational signs have been attached to the trees at strategic locations. Historical tours are also conducted a few times a year by a local historian. The forest preserve district also plans to further develop the site by building an

Statues of Marquette, Jolliet, and a Native American, Chicago Portage National Historic Site

interpretive center. In addition, the City of Chicago and the Chicago Park District are in the process of developing another interpretive site called the Canal Origins Site Park at the east end of the portage next to the south branch of the Chicago River, where the east end of the Illinois and Michigan Canal began.

REGULATIONS: All items are protected by law.

HOURS: The site closes at sunset.

DIRECTIONS: From I-55, go north on Harlem Avenue (exit 283) for .5 mile; the entrance is on the west side of the street.

CONTACT INFORMATION: Forest Preserve District of Cook County, Cummings Square, 536 N. Harlem Ave., River Forest, IL 60305; (773) 261-8400 (city); (708) 366-9420 (suburbs); TTY (708) 771-1190

38.   Little Red Schoolhouse Nature Center

HIGHLIGHTS:
- *Historic one-room log cabin schoolhouse*
- *Environmental learning center*
- *Hands-on exhibits and displays*
- *Outdoor education staff*
- *Part of the Palos Forest Preserves*

PROGRAMS AND EVENTS:
- *Winter Sky*
- *Cook County Critters*
- *Birds of Prey*
- *Night hike*
- *Arts and crafts fair*
- *Children's nature tales*
- *Nature walk*

DESCRIPTION: The Little Red Schoolhouse Nature Center is part of the Palos Forest Preserve in Cook County. The most popular trail from the nature center is the .25-mile **Farm Pond Trail** that loops around the southwestern side of the center. There are rest stops and observation blinds along this trail. At the west end of the trail is a junction with the **Black Oak Trail,** where the original schoolhouse site was. The **White Oak Trail** (a 1-mile loop) is directly across the parking lot (south) from the nature center. All of the trails allow the visitor to experience the diversity of the plant life in this region. The brochures available at the park describe the history of development and changes to the area. The trails have dirt and wood-chip surfaces and can be enjoyed year-round.

REGULATIONS: Remain on trails. Do not remove anything.

HOURS: March–October—parking lot and trails are open weekdays, 8:00 AM–5:00 PM, and weekends, 8:00 AM–5:30 PM; exhibit building is open Monday–Thursday, 9:00 AM–4:30 PM, and weekends, 9:00 AM–5:00 PM. November–February—parking lot and trails are open daily, 8:00 AM–4:30 PM; exhibit building is open Saturday–Thursday, 9:00 AM–4:00 PM. The grounds are closed on Thanksgiving, Christmas, and New Year's Day.

Schoolyard interpretive sign, Little Red Schoolhouse Nature Center

DIRECTIONS: From I-55, go south on US 45 (96th Avenue), turn west on 95th Street, and go south on 104th Avenue (Willow Springs Road) to the entrance on the right.

CONTACT INFORMATION: Little Red Schoolhouse Nature Center, 9800 S. Willow Springs Rd., Willow Springs, IL 60480; (708) 839-6897

39. Lake Katherine Nature Preserve

HIGHLIGHTS:

- *Environmental learning center*
- *Clubhouse*
- *Wetlands*
- *Waterfall*
- *Children's forest*

- *Exhibits*
- *Observation decks*
- *Ice skating rink*
- *Wildflower garden*
- *Arboretum*
- *Staff naturalist*

PROGRAMS AND EVENTS:

- *School programs*
- *Scout programs*
- *Programs for seniors*

- *Programs for families*
- *Programs for the disabled*

DESCRIPTION: Lake Katherine Nature Preserve is in Palos Heights (Cook County). There is a clubhouse available for functions and a nature center with exhibits as well as a small gift shop. Classes and education programs are held at the nature center. The preserve is divided into western and eastern sections divided by Harlem Avenue. The western preserve is visited more often because it contains the clubhouse, the learning center, and Lake Katherine. The **Lake Katherine Trail** is a 1-mile loop around the lake. There is a canal overlook just west of the learning center. At the west end of the lake is **Birders Trail,** a .25-mile spur trail (one way). Following the Lake Katherine Trail east past the clubhouse is the connecting trail to the eastern preserve. The **Old Canoe Path Trail** and the **Overlook Trail** are mile-long, one-way trails in the eastern preserve. The .12-mile **Bottomland Loop Trail** at the far east end of the preserve crosses over Navajo Creek. Most of the trail surfaces are wood chip and dirt and can be enjoyed year-round.

REGULATIONS: Remain on trails. Do not remove anything. No picnicking, alcohol, radios, or campfires allowed. No blankets allowed on grass. Use benches.

HOURS: The preserve is open daily, dawn to 10:00 PM; the learning center is open daily except holidays.

DIRECTIONS: From I-55, go south on US 45 (96th Street), turn east on IL 83 to Lake Katherine Drive, about .25 mile west of Harlem Avenue.

CONTACT INFORMATION: Environmental Learning Center, 7402 Lake Katherine Dr., Palos Heights, IL 60463; (708) 361-1873

40.   Sand Ridge Nature Center

HIGHLIGHTS:
- *Nature center with exhibit room*
- *Classroom for outdoor education*
- *Seasonal outdoor exhibits*
- *Butterfly garden*
- *Vegetable garden*
- *Reconstructed pioneer log cabins*

PROGRAMS AND EVENTS:
- *Birds of Prey*
- *Fall Prairie Prowl*
- *Regularly scheduled audiovisual programs*
- *Special education programs for teachers*
- *Guided walks*
- *Demonstrations*
- *Night hike*
- *Children's nature tales*
- *Bird feeder workshop*
- *Do-it-yourself night hike*

DESCRIPTION: The Sand Ridge Nature Center in South Holland (Cook County) provides educational and recreational opportunities and features an exhibit room that houses displays, activities, and examples of native wildlife. The **Redwing Trail** is a .5-mile loop directly north of the center. It has lettered posts (A–I) with an accompanying guide brochure available at the center. This short trail offers a good exposure to the forests, shrubs, prairie grasses, and aquatic features of the region. Other trails feature overlooks and observation points as well as a greater variety of plants and wildlife. Most of the trail surfaces are mowed grass or compacted dirt.

REGULATIONS: Remain on trails. Do not remove anything. No pets or bicycles allowed on trails.

HOURS: March–October—parking lot and trails inside of gates are open weekdays, 8:00 AM–5:00 PM, and weekends and holidays, 8:00 AM–5:30 PM; exhibit building and trails outside of gates are open weekdays, 9:00 AM–4:30 PM, and weekends and holidays, 9:00 AM–5:00 PM. November–February—parking lot and trails inside of gates are open daily, 8:00 AM–4:30 PM; exhibit building and trails outside of gates are open daily, 9:00 AM–4:00 PM.

Reconstructed pioneer log cabin, Sand Ridge Nature Center

DIRECTIONS: From I-94 in South Holland, take 159th Street (US 6) east for 1 mile to Paxton Avenue, turn left (north), and travel .5 mile to the sign and entrance on the right.

CONTACT INFORMATION: Sand Ridge Nature Center, Forest Preserve District of Cook County, 15890 Paxton Ave., South Holland, IL 60473; (708) 868-0606, TDD (708) 771-1190

41.   Albany Mounds State Historic Site

HIGHLIGHTS:
- *Largest Hopewell Native American culture site in Illinois*
- *Nearly 50 burial mounds*
- *Site listed on the National Register of Historic Places*
- *Restored prairie*
- *Component of the Grand Illinois Trail*
- *Interpretive trail*

DESCRIPTION: Albany Mounds State Historic Site, on bluffs overlooking the Mississippi River floodplain in Whiteside County, is a remarkable 200-acre site that was occupied by Native Americans for over 10,000 years. Originally, the site contained over 90 mounds built by people of the Hopewell Culture; today, nearly 50 are still preserved by the state. The Hopewell are known for their pottery and other trade goods as well as their burial mounds. A local group, the Friends of Albany Mounds Foundation, has been instrumental in preserving and developing trails at the site. Today, visitors get a great chance to explore many of the mounds by following over 2 miles of trails, which also

Native American mound, Albany Mounds State Historic Site

feature tree and flower interpretive signs. A paved component of the **Grand Illinois Trail** allows bicyclists to ride the paved trail through the site and then walk the grass trails throughout the grounds. A restored prairie at the complex enables visitors to gain an appreciation for how Illinois once looked.

REGULATIONS: No horseback riding, snowmobiling, flower picking, or hunting permitted. The site is protected by law.

HOURS: The site is open daily, sunrise to sunset.

DIRECTIONS: From I-80, go north on IL 84 (exit 7) for 17 miles into Albany. Turn right on South Park Avenue and go 2 blocks to Church Street. Turn north, go half a block, and then turn east on Fifth Avenue. Go up the hill, turn south at Cherry Street, and follow it for .5 mile to the parking lot at the sign for Albany Mounds.

CONTACT INFORMATION: Friends of the Indian Mounds Foundation, PO Box 512, Albany, IL 61230; (309) 887-4335

42. Lowell Park

HIGHLIGHTS:
- *Nature center with various hands-on exhibits, displays, and information*
- *8 trails totaling over 5 miles in length*
- *Rock River*
- *Park where President Ronald Reagan was a lifeguard*
- Nuthatch News *newsletter*
- *Oak-hickory forest*
- *Wildflowers*

PROGRAMS AND EVENTS:
- *Spring wildflower walks*
- *Family campfires*
- *Nature camps*
- *Astronomy nights*
- *Slide shows*

DESCRIPTION: Lowell Park Nature Center, on 240 acres of wooded terrain overlooking the beautiful Rock River, is the second largest park within the Dixon Park District of Lee County. As a teenager, former president Ronald Reagan served here as a lifeguard, reportedly saving a number of lives from the swift current of the river. The nature center has many hands-on exhibits, displays, and programs. In addition, there is a series of 8 trails totaling over 5 miles. All the trails are interconnected and wind their way through the site. The **Shagbark Trail, Pedestrian Trail,** and **Quarry Trail** begin near the nature center, and each is marked with a wooden sign at the trailhead. Connecting trails lead to the Rock River and some nice views of the river valley. Interesting limestone rock outcrops are seen along the west side of the Quarry Trail, and wildflowers may be seen throughout the park. Keep your eyes open for animals such as deer or fox and the many species of birds. Some portions of these trails are steep, slippery, or otherwise hazardous.

REGULATIONS: Carry out all items brought into the park. No guns, loudspeakers, or alcoholic beverages allowed. Use grills only. Do not collect any plant or animal materials.

HOURS: The park is open for pedestrians from sunrise to sunset; for vehicle traffic, 7:00 AM to sunset (weather permitting). The nature center is open daily, 1:00 – 4:00 PM, Memorial Day to Labor Day; and weekends, 1:00 – 4:00 PM, in winter.

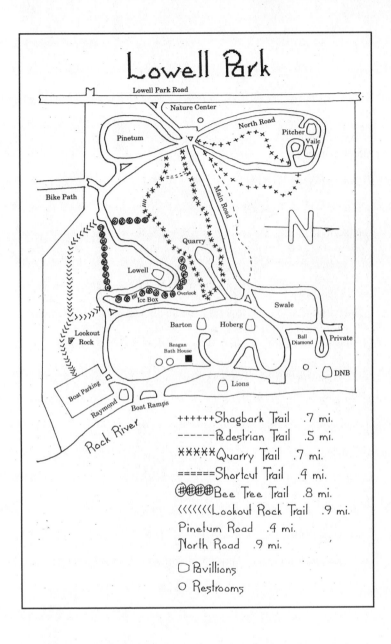

Lowell Park

Lowell Park Road

Nature Center

Pinetum

North Road

Pitcher

Vaile

Bike Path

Main Road

Quarry

Lowell

Ice Box

Overlook

Swale

Lookout Rock

Barton

Hoberg

Reagan Bath House

Ball Diamond

Private

Boat Parking

Lions

DNB

Raymond

Boat Ramps

Rock River

++++++Shagbark Trail   .7 mi.
------Pedestrian Trail   .5 mi.
✗✗✗✗✗Quarry Trail   .7 mi.
======Shortcut Trail   .4 mi.
⊕⊕⊕⊕Bee Tree Trail   .8 mi.
‹‹‹‹‹‹‹Lookout Rock Trail   .9 mi.
Pinetum Road   .4 mi.
North Road   .9 mi.

⬭ Pavillions
○ Restrooms

DIRECTIONS: From I-88 (the East-West Tollway), take IL 26 into Dixon. At the north end of town, turn north (right) on Lowell Park Road and go 2.2 miles to the park entrance on the east side of the road.

CONTACT INFORMATION: Lowell Park Nature Center, 2114 Lowell Park Rd., Dixon, IL 61021; (815) 288-5209. Dixon Park District, 804 Palmyra Ave., Dixon, IL 61021; (815) 284-3306; www.dixonil.com/parks   63

43.   Page Park

HIGHLIGHTS:
- *Interpretive trail*
- *Upland forest*
- *Rock River views*

DESCRIPTION: Page Park is operated by the Dixon Park District of Lee County along the Rock River, a few miles from where former president Ronald Reagan grew up. The interpretive **Plum Creek Trail** is a 1-mile, wood-chip trail and has 20 numbered wooden posts, leading visitors beside Plum Creek to the Rock River. The trail then parallels the river for a short distance, taking visitors up a small hill and into an upland forest of hardwoods with numerous wildflowers and songbirds, down one hill and up another to an abandoned railroad grade. When the foliage is bare, there are views of the Rock River floodplain. The trail then turns to the right where it comes to an end at an old railroad trestle and viewing area. Visitors turn around and head along the railroad bed down to Everett Street and back to the starting point or double back along the trail. A brochure is available at the trailhead.

REGULATIONS: Stay on trail.

HOURS: The park is open only during daylight for safety.

DIRECTIONS: From I-88 (the East-West Tollway), take IL 26 north into Dixon. On the north side of the Rock River, turn west at Everett Street and go .8 mile to Page Park, on the left side of the road. Turn left at the park entrance and park at the tennis courts next to Everett Street. The trail begins near Everett, where a trail sign may be seen.

CONTACT INFORMATION: Dixon Park District, 804 Palmyra St., Dixon, IL 61021; (815) 284-3306; dixonil.com/parks

44.   Franklin Creek State Natural Area

HIGHLIGHTS:
- *520-acre natural area*
- *Mill Springs*
- *Rock outcroppings*
- *96-acre Illinois Nature Preserve*
- *Franklin Creek*
- *Numerous species of game and other wildlife*

DESCRIPTION: Franklin Creek State Natural Area in Lee County is an outstanding and diverse natural area in a beautiful setting. The concrete-surfaced **Mill Springs Accessible Trail** is suitable for people of all mobility levels. The .3-mile, one-way trail leads from the picnic shelter and parking area to Mill Springs. Along the way there are picnic tables and rest stops. At Mill Springs itself there is a fishing pier designed for individuals with disabilities. A wide variety of flora and fauna may be seen in this small river valley. Spring, summer, and fall are all good times to visit.

REGULATIONS: All pets must be leashed.

HOURS: The site is open daily except Christmas and New Year's Day.

Trailhead sign, Franklin Creek State Natural Area

65

DIRECTIONS: From I-88 (the East-West Tollway), take IL 26 into Dixon and head east on IL 38 (7th Street) about 2 miles. Turn north on Twist Road and go 1 mile to Old Mill Road. Turn right (east) to the entrance.

CONTACT INFORMATION: Site Superintendent, Franklin Creek State Natural Area, 1872 Twist Rd., Franklin Grove, IL 61031; (815) 456-2878; www.dnr.state.il.us/lands/landmgt/parks/r1/franklin.htm

45.   Spring Brook Nature Center

HIGHLIGHTS:
- *Nature center with various exhibits, Children's Discovery Room, books, and fish*
- *Raptor program*
- *Birds of prey in outdoor viewing cages*
- *Arboretum*
- *Wildflowers*
- *700-foot boardwalk over marsh*
- *Marsh/wetland complex*

PROGRAMS AND EVENTS:
- *Junior naturalist program*
- *Hikes for Tykes*
- *Kids 'n' Critters*
- *Wildland Explorers*
- *Wild Ones Club*
- *Discovery Trail Packs (self-guided nature activities)*
- *Arbor Day celebration*
- *Summer day camps*
- *Animal care camp*
- *Nature bird day camp*
- *Nature neighbors day camp*
- *Classes for schools, Scouts, and other youth groups*

DESCRIPTION: Spring Brook Nature Center in Itasca (DuPage County) is a 63-acre nature center, marsh/wetland complex, and arboretum. The nature center specializes in rehabilitation and fieldwork with live raptors. An internship program and school programs are available. The park also has 2 miles of wood-chip trails and a boardwalk. The trails lead the visitor past outdoor raptor cages, through a meadow, over Spring Brook Creek to a wooded area, to an arboretum where the various tree species are labeled, over to a gazebo for a view of the marsh, and onto a 700-foot boardwalk over the marsh/wetland, where numerous bird species may be seen. At times the trail may be inundated, so prepare accordingly.

REGULATIONS: Leash all dogs and pick up trash. No swimming or wading allowed. Supervise children on the boardwalk.

Staff member with falcon, Spring Brook Nature Center

HOURS: The grounds are open daily, sunrise to sunset. The nature center is open Tuesday–Sunday, 11:00 AM–5:00 PM, June–August; and 1:00–5:00 PM, September–May; closed on Mondays and holidays.

DIRECTIONS: From I-290, go west on Thorndale (exit 5) for .5 mile to Rohlwing Road. Turn south and go 3 miles to Irving Park Road. Turn east, go past I-290, and turn south on Maple Street. Continue 1 block to Grove Street, turn west, and go 2 blocks to the nature center. Access to the park is also available from Irving Park at Catalpa Street. Go south on Catalpa, past the public library and the water park. There is a trailhead at the south end of the parking lot leading over a bridge to the nature center.

CONTACT INFORMATION: Spring Brook Nature Center, 130 Forest Ave., Itasca, IL 60143; (630) 773-5572; www.itasca.com/nature/itnat.htm

46. Spring Creek Reservoir Forest Preserve

HIGHLIGHTS:
- *Accessible trail*
- *Fishing*
- *Bird-watching*

DESCRIPTION: Spring Creek Reservoir Forest Preserve, near Blooming-dale in DuPage County, was built as a water storage unit to hold excess floodwaters from Springbrook Creek. The site is also a recreation area, and a multipurpose, 1-mile, paved, accessible trail circles the reservoir. The trail passes over the spillway and through some wooded areas where numerous bird species may be seen. Benches are provided along the trail, and a trail spur leads down to the lake (foot traffic only).

REGULATIONS: Ground fires and alcohol are prohibited. Leash pets. No hunting, trapping, or swimming permitted. No removal of plants, animals, rocks, fossils, or artifacts allowed.

HOURS: The preserve is open 1 hour after sunrise to 1 hour after sunset.

DIRECTIONS: From I-355, take Lake Street (US 20) west for 1.5 miles. The park entrance is on the north side of the road.

CONTACT INFORMATION: Forest Preserve District of DuPage County, PO Box 2329, Glen Ellyn, IL 60138; (630) 933-7200; TTY (800) 526-0857; www.dupageforest.com/preserves/springcreekreservoir.html

47.   Springfield Park Nature Area

HIGHLIGHTS:
- *Accessible trail*
- *Interpretive signs*
- *Wetlands/marsh area*
- *Prairie*
- *Boardwalk with observation deck*

DESCRIPTION: The Springfield Park Nature Area is a 20-acre parcel in the 51-acre Springfield Park complex in Bloomingdale (DuPage County). The site consists of a restored wetland/detention pond and marsh area, as well as a prairie, in addition to other recreation facilities. A 1.1-mile, paved, interpretive trail goes around the 2 ponds, which are connected by a wooden bridge and boardwalk providing good views of the wetlands. Numerous bird species may be seen, as well as the many bird houses built for them. Thirty glass-encased interpretive signs placed around the trail describe prairies, wetlands, plants, birds, and other natural features of the site. Family night activities are held at the nature area between April and September of each year.

REGULATIONS: No swimming, fishing, or camping permitted. Leash all pets and pick up after them. Keep pets on trail.

HOURS: The site closes at sunset.

DIRECTIONS: From I-355, head west on Army Trail Road for 2.5 miles to Bloomingdale Road. Turn north and go 1.2 miles to Schick Road. Turn west and go .7 mile to the park entrance on the north side of the road. Access to the nature area is via the path through the baseball fields.

CONTACT INFORMATION: Bloomingdale Park District, 172 S. Circle Ave., Bloomingdale, IL 60108; (630) 529-3650; www.bdalenature.org

48.   Lincoln Marsh Natural Area

HIGHLIGHTS:
- *Open marsh/wetland complex*
- *Prairies, woodlands, and oak savanna*
- *Trail connection to the Illinois Prairie Path*
- *Boardwalk*
- *Observation deck*

DESCRIPTION: Lincoln Marsh Natural Area is a 131-acre complex in Wheaton (DuPage County). Found at the site are wetlands, prairies, a small woodland, and a savanna. A series of loop trails lead through the various ecological zones; some large oaks and cottonwoods are seen along the way. A wood-chip path crosses the southern portion of the site. A leg of this trail also leads up a set of accessible stairs to a marsh overlook with an interpretive sign and a good view of the wetland complex. A separate crushed-limestone trail in the northern section leads from the **Illinois Prairie Path** (a 55-mile, multiuse trail), where a wood deck and a Lincoln Marsh interpretive sign may be seen, to a shelter and finally to Harrison Street. A teams and rope course is also found in the northwest part of the grounds.

Interpretive sign and observation deck, Lincoln Marsh Natural Area

REGULATIONS: Leash all pets. Bikes are prohibited on wood-chip trails. No alcohol permitted. All plants and animals are protected. Teams and rope course to be used only under park supervision.

HOURS: The site closes at dark.

DIRECTIONS: Take IL 64 to County Farm Road in Wheaton. Head south for 2.6 miles to Harrison Avenue. Turn east and proceed .9 mile to the parking area.

CONTACT INFORMATION: Wheaton Park District, 666 S. Main St., Wheaton, IL 60181; (630) 871-2810; www.wheatonparkdistrict.com/parks/lincoln_marsh.html

49.   Willowbrook Wildlife Center

HIGHLIGHTS:
- *Wildlife rehabilitation and education center*
- *30 species of wildlife*
- *Outdoor animal exhibits*
- *Various exhibits, gifts, and hands-on activities*
- *Restored prairie*
- *Accessible and nature/interpretive trails*

PROGRAMS AND EVENTS:
- *Naturalist-led programs (e.g., tracking, wildlife habitat and survival, raptors)*
- *Young Explorers*
- *Hodge Podge Lodge*
- *Birds of prey*
- *Roger Raccoon Club*
- *Tours (e.g., birds of prey, mammal tracking, sensory awareness, ecology and wildlife management)*

DESCRIPTION: Willowbrook Wildlife Center, in Glen Ellyn (DuPage County), is a rehabilitation center for injured and orphaned wildlife. The facility includes the rehabilitation center and education center, an outdoor animal exhibit area, and nature trails. The trails total .75 mile in length with paved and packed gravel surfaces. Picnic facilities and a shelter are at the parking area. Inside the wildlife center are various exhibits, windows to view injured wildlife being cared for, a hands-on museum, and a slide show. Books, binoculars, decals, and other materials may also be purchased at the center. Two loop trails allow visitors to explore the grounds. A short, paved trail outside the center takes the visitor by cages where foxes, owls, hawks, groundhogs, and raccoons may be seen. It then connects with a loop trail on the east side of Glen Crest Creek. Along this packed gravel trail is a small marsh and exhibit, a restored prairie, and a plant succession and geology exhibit.

REGULATIONS: Leash all pets. Alcohol is prohibited.

HOURS: The site is open daily, 9:00 AM–5:00 PM.

DIRECTIONS: From I-355, head west on Roosevelt Road (about 1 mile) or Butterfield Road (a little over 2 miles) to Park Boulevard. From

Roosevelt Road, turn south on Park and travel 1 mile to the entrance on the east side of the road; from Butterfield Road, go north 1 mile on Park.

CONTACT INFORMATION: Willowbrook Wildlife Center, Park Blvd. at 22nd Street, Glen Ellyn, IL 60137; (630) 942-6200; www.dupageforest .com/education/willowbrook.html

50.   Elmhurst Great Western Prairie

HIGHLIGHTS:
- *Restored prairie and wildflower area*
- *Interpretive trail*
- *Interpretive prairie garden*
- *Access to the Illinois Prairie Path*

DESCRIPTION: Although surrounded by residential development, the Great Western Prairie in Elmhurst (DuPage County) is one of the few original prairies found along the **Illinois Prairie Path** and offers more than 85 plant species on 6 acres of grounds. The **Shooting Star Trail** circles the prairie and parallels the Illinois Prairie Path to the south. The trail is 1.5 miles in length and consists of dirt, grass, and packed gravel. It has 17 numbered stations corresponding to descriptions found in a guide and map available at the trailhead. Some of the plants that may be seen include big bluestem, goldenrod, rattlesnake master, and pale prairie coneflower, as well as shooting star. At the west end of the trail is Salt Creek and a trail board along the Illinois Prairie Path. Spring through late fall is the best time to visit.

Day lily on the Shooting Star Trail, Elmhurst Great Western Prairie

REGULATIONS: No picking of flowers allowed.

HOURS: The site is open only during daylight for safety.

DIRECTIONS: From IL 83 in Elmhurst, turn east on St. Charles Road and travel .7 mile to Spring Road. Turn south and go .3 mile to a parking lot along the trail; parking is also available on the street.

CONTACT INFORMATION: Elmhurst Park District, 225 Prospect Ave., Elmhurst, IL 60126; (630) 993-8900; www.epd.org/egwp.htm

51. Lake View Nature Center

HIGHLIGHTS:

- *Animal displays*
- *Nature center*
- *Nature exhibits*
- *Restored prairie*
- *Wetland exploration*
- *Wildlife conservation*
- *Accessible trail*

PROGRAMS AND EVENTS:

- *Group programs for environmental education*
- *Nature programs*
- *Scout programs*
- *Halloween Night Hike*
- *Spooky Spiders*
- *Turkey Time*
- *Coyote: Little Wolf on the Prairie*
- *Insect Safari*
- *Animal Adventures*
- *Turtle Talk*
- *Going Batty*
- *Tree trimming party*
- *Family rock climbing*

DESCRIPTION: Lake View Nature Center in Oakbrook Terrace (DuPage County), nestled in an oasis between residential, commercial, and retail property, offers educational opportunities, displays, and a knowledgeable staff. A .4-mile loop trail that follows the perimeter of the pond is a popular walking and exercise path partly consisting of crushed rock and partly concrete paved. Along the way, the visitor can view a prairie restoration project, enjoy the neighboring Terrace View Park, and see the occasional angler catching "a big one." Spring, summer, and fall are good times to visit.

HOURS: Open Monday–Friday, 9:00 AM–4:00 PM.

DIRECTIONS: From I-88 (the East-West Tollway, go north on IL 83. Cross 22nd Avenue and turn left (west) at the next stoplight, Hodges Road, and look for the sign for Terrace View Park.

CONTACT INFORMATION: Lake View Nature Center, 17 W. 063 Hodges Rd., Oakbrook Terrace, IL 60181; (630) 941-8747

52.   York Woods Forest Preserve

HIGHLIGHTS:
- *Accessible trail*
- *Wooded parcel*

DESCRIPTION: York Woods Forest Preserve in Glen Ellyn was the first area purchased by the Forest Preserve District of DuPage County. The famous Illinois poet Carl Sandburg once lived on this property. Today, the forest preserve has picnic shelters, water pumps, latrines, and a 1-mile, paved, accessible trail comprised of a large loop and a small loop that wind their way between the south and north access areas of the preserve.

REGULATIONS: Ground fires and alcohol are prohibited. Leash pets. No hunting or trapping allowed. No removal of plants or animals, rocks, fossils, or other artifacts permitted.

HOURS: The preserve is open 1 hour after sunrise to 1 hour after sunset.

DIRECTIONS: From I-290, go west on St. Charles Road (exit 14) to York Road, turn south, and continue a few blocks south of Roosevelt Road (IL 38). The entrance is on the west side of the road. Turn west and go 1 block to a stop sign and the highway frontage road. The south access to the park can be reached by going left at the stop sign for a few blocks to the parking area. The north access area can be reached by going right on the frontage road for .6 mile.

CONTACT INFORMATION: Forest Preserve District of DuPage County, PO Box 2329, Glen Ellyn, IL 60138; (630) 933-7200; TTY (800) 526-0857; www.dupageforest.com/preserves/yorkwoods.html

53.   Blackwell Forest Preserve

- *Accessible trail*
- *Views of Silver Lake*
- *Numerous recreation facilities*
- *Fishing and boating opportunities*
- *Bird-watching opportunities*

DESCRIPTION: Blackwell Forest Preserve in DuPage County is a 1,311-acre park broken into northern and southern sections, with the developed recreation areas in the southern section off Butterfield Road. Nearly 8 miles of trails are found within the preserve, including a short connecting trail segment to the Illinois Prairie Path. The accessible, .5-mile, paved, loop trail is a good way to see part of the preserve and to explore Silver Lake. It begins east of the boat launch/concession area and winds past a few small picnic areas back to the staring point. A trail board, benches, accessible fishing pier, and picnic tables are found along the trail.

REGULATIONS: No swimming permitted. A boat launch permit is required.

Fishing from an accessible pier, Blackwell Forest Preserve

79

HOURS: The preserve is open 1 hour after sunrise to 1 hour after sunset.

DIRECTIONS: From I-88 (the East-West Tollway), take the Winfield Road exit. Head north for 1.7 miles to Butterfield Road. Turn west and go .4 mile to the park entrance on the north side of the road. Proceed .6 mile to the parking area for the boat launch.

CONTACT INFORMATION: Forest Preserve District of DuPage County, 185 Spring Ave., PO Box 2339, Glen Ellyn, IL 60138; (630) 790-4900; www.dupageforest.com/preserves/blackwell.html

54.   Morton Arboretum

HIGHLIGHTS:
- *1,700-acre arboretum*
- *3,600 trees, shrubs, and vines from around the world*
- *Restored prairies*
- *Visitor center, restaurant, and gift shop*
- *12 miles of trails, including accessible and interpretive trails*
- *Woodlands and wetlands*
- Seasons *newsletter*
- *Tour bus (seasonal)*

PROGRAMS AND EVENTS:
- *Nature explorers programs (grades K–8)*
- *Leafing Through the Arboretum*
- *Guided Walks*
- *Summer Children's Walk*
- *Animals after Dark*
- *Family Overnight Arboretum Style*
- *Little School on the Prairie*
- *200 classes, workshops, and field trips*
- *Certificate degrees (naturalist, home landscape horticulture, botanical art and illustration)*
- *Landscape workshops*
- *Arbor Day celebration*
- *Annual nature artists spring show*
- *Tram tours*
- *Family campfire and night hike*
- *Fall harvest feast*
- *Special lecture series*

DESCRIPTION: The Morton Arboretum in Lisle (DuPage County) is a research and education facility offering a tranquil experience in an urban setting 25 miles from downtown Chicago. The property was once owned by Joy Morton, the founder of the Morton Salt Company, who began to develop an arboretum in 1921. Today, the 1,700-acre facility hosts workshops, field trips, and other programs. Over 12 miles of trails and footpaths allow visitors a chance to view many of the gardens, research areas, ponds, wetlands, restored prairies, and woodlands, as well as the more than 41,000 plants, including 3,700 trees, shrubs, and vines.

*Family explor-
ing nature,
Morton
Arboretum*

Also on the grounds are a visitor center, gift shop, and restaurant. Visitors receive a map and guide after paying an entrance fee to the grounds. A few of the interpretive and accessible trails are described here.

The **Illinois Trees Trail, Loop 1,** outside the visitor center, is a good place to start. This paved, accessible trail makes its way around Meadow Lake for .6 mile. Along the trail are benches and metal markers that identify the tree species. The trail goes through a stand of pines.

The **Heritage Trail** is a relatively new, self-guided, interpretive trail just over 1 mile in length on a wood-chip surface. The trail is at the eastern end of the property and begins at parking lot 14. Nine numbered stations along this loop guide visitors through a white oak woodland, a marsh, and a savanna and past a glacial rock and an old saw mill site. A beautiful stand of bur oak and white oak can be seen between stations 5 and 6. A Heritage Trail brochure is available at the visitor center.

The **Joy Path,** on the west side of IL 53, begins at the Thornhill Education Center, which once served as the home of Joy Morton. The trail passes through the Fragrance Garden and then along a paved, accessible, .5-mile path through some flower gardens.

A .5-mile interpretive trail is also found in the Schulenberg Prairie on the southwest side of the arboretum, where numerous prairie plants may be seen.

REGULATIONS: No bikes, pets, fishing, hunting, trapping, intoxicants, or damaging of plants permitted. Grills and fires prohibited. Park in numbered lots only.

HOURS: The grounds are open daily, 7:00 AM–7:00 PM, Daylight Savings Time; 7:00 AM–5:00 PM, Central Standard Time. The visitor center, gift shop, and coffee shop are open daily, 9:00 AM–5:00 PM.

DIRECTIONS: From eastbound I-88 (the East-West Tollway), turn onto I-355 and exit at Ogden Avenue. Head west for 1.3 miles to IL 53 and travel north for 1 mile to the entrance. From westbound I-88, exit at IL 53 north to the grounds.

CONTACT INFORMATION: The Morton Arboretum, 4100 Illinois Route 53, Lisle, IL 60532-1293; (630) 719-2400; www.mortonarb.org

55. Fullersburg Woods Environmental Education Center

HIGHLIGHTS:

- *Historic Graue Mill, listed as a National Historic Landmark*
- *Visitor center with various exhibits and programs*
- *Salt Creek*
- *Interpretive, accessible, and multiuse trails*
- *Staff naturalist*
- *Wildflowers*

PROGRAMS AND EVENTS:

- *Various educational programs (e.g., Learn to Be a Nature Detective, Trees Please!, From Grass to Hawks, Migration Headache, Maple Syrup, Changes, Biodiversity Workday, Dig Dem Bones)*
- *In-school programs (e.g., Wildlife and You, Animals in Danger, Winter Animals)*
- *Nature Quest*
- *Teacher training*
- *Weekday bird walks*

DESCRIPTION: Fullersburg Woods Environmental Education Center, operated by the Forest Preserve District of DuPage County in Oak Brook, is on a site filled with history. The Potawatomi tribe once inhabited the area, and early settlers used the creek for ice-making operations as well as for powering their grist mill. As the population began to grow and industrial sources sprang up along the creek, various pollutants contaminated the water, which became so polluted that Fullersburg was closed for 3 years in the early 1970s. Today, after years of reducing water pollution, the area is making a comeback as birds and other wildlife return. The grounds consist of floodplain forest along both sides of Salt Creek, a visitor center and environmental education center, the historic Graue Mill, and multipurpose trails, three of which are described here. Many outdoor programs for the public and for teachers are offered by the staff naturalists.

The **Interpretive Trail** leads north from the visitor center and consists of 2 loops totaling 1.3 miles in length. Along the trail are various interpretive signs mounted on old utility poles describing the local flora and fauna. The trail goes past Salt Creek and leads to a small wildlife island; pets are prohibited there. The Interpretive Trail connects with many of the other park trails, and the trail surface is packed gravel.

Historic Graue Mill, Fullersburg Woods Environmental Education Center

The **Wildflower Trail** is a short, gravel trail west of the visitor center that leads through a planted wildflower area.

The **Trail to Graue Mill** is on the west side of Salt Creek and leads south from the visitor center to the mill and parking area. The trail is .5 mile long and is paved. Along the trail are views of Salt Creek and various interpretive signs. For those who prefer, a bicycle can be taken on the path. The mill was built in 1852 and is operated by the nonprofit DuPage Graue Mill Corporation. On the east side of Salt Creek is a multipurpose trail that leads back to the park.

REGULATIONS: Leash all pets. Alcoholic beverages prohibited. Stay on designated trails. No collecting of plants or animals allowed.

HOURS: The visitor center is open daily, 9:00 AM–5:00 PM. The grounds are open 1 hour after sunrise to 1 hour after sunset. Graue Mill is open daily, mid-April–mid-November, 10:00 AM–4:30PM.

DIRECTIONS: From I-294 (the Tri-State Tollway), exit at Ogden Avenue and head west to York Road. Turn north and head for .3 mile to Spring Road. Turn west and go 1 mile to the park entrance on the right side of the road. From IL 83 in Oak Brook, turn east on 31st and travel .6 mile to Spring Road. Turn south and travel .9 mile to the park entrance on the north side of the road.

CONTACT INFORMATION: Fullersburg Woods Forest Preserve, 3609 Spring Rd., Oak Brook, IL 60521; (630) 850-8110; www.dupageforest.com/education/fullersburg.html

56.   Lyman Woods Natural Area

HIGHLIGHTS:
- *Illinois Nature Preserve*
- *17-acre oak savanna*
- *Native prairie*
- *Marsh*
- *Over 300 species of native plants*

PROGRAMS AND EVENTS:
- *Guided group tours*
- *Outdoor education through local schools*

DESCRIPTION: Lyman Woods is in Downers Grove (DuPage County). The trail system is comprised of 4 connecting loops having brown posts and markers with the universal hiker symbol and arrows for direction. The trails total 2 miles and consist of dirt and mowed grass. The first loop trail passes through .12 mile of open field and then crosses a marsh and pond via a boardwalk. It then heads east, where an observation pier is available for viewing north across the pond. Continuing past the pier, there is a connecting loop trail passing through several acres of oak woods. After completing the oak woods loop, the trail meanders east out of the preserve and onto the Midwestern University property for

Visitor at trail junction, Lyman Woods Natural Area

.12 mile north and then heads back west across a marsh. Approximately .5 mile after reentering the preserve from the university property, there is another trail junction. Continuing west, the hiker approaches more oak woods and open fields and then retraces the route back to the parking area. Heading north from this trail junction there are 2 newer loop trails. The northeasternmost trail passes around an open meadow, while the northwesternmost loop passes through a huge oak forest; it also has steep grades and some challenging climbs. Future preserve plans include an on-site nature center.

REGULATIONS: Remain on trails. Do not remove anything.

HOURS: The site is open daily, sunrise to sunset.

DIRECTIONS: From I-355, take the Ogden Avenue exit and head east for 2.25 miles to Highland Avenue. Turn north and go 1 mile to the parking area on the east side of the road.

CONTACT INFORMATION: Downers Grove Park District, 2455 Warrenville Rd., Downers Grove, IL 60515-1726; (630) 963-1304

57.   Black Hawk State Historic Site

HIGHLIGHTS:
- *Hauberg Indian Museum*
- *Black Hawk Prairie*
- *Rock River*
- *Hardwood forest*
- *Spring wildflowers (over 30 species)*
- *106-acre Illinois Nature Preserve with 4 miles of trails*
- *Dickson Pioneer Cemetery*
- *Interpretive trail*
- *Black Hawk statue*

PROGRAMS AND EVENTS:
- *Programs on bald eagles, prairies, trees, and mammals*
- *September prairie program*
- *Geology and archaeology programs*
- *Stroll Through Springtime bird and wildflower hikes*
- *Moonlight Walk on Valentine's Day*
- *Black Hawk Days*

DESCRIPTION: Black Hawk State Historic Site is in Rock Island County along the Rock River. The 208-acre site was occupied for over 12,000 years by Native Americans, although the area is best known for the Sauk tribe and the warrior chief Black Hawk. The park includes a wooded area along the river, as well as a rolling nature preserve on the north side of Black Hawk Road (IL 5). Spring wildflowers abound here and the native hardwood forest is striking. The Hauberg Indian Museum, lodge, park office, a 1.3-mile interpretive trail, and prairie are found along the south side of Black Hawk Road. Within the museum are various exhibits depicting Native American life, replicas of Sauk houses, and a canoe. Many of the museum pieces were donated by Dr. John Hauberg.

The 1.3-mile, interpretive **Rock River Trail** offers a little bit of everything, from wildflowers to Rock River views, a floodplain forest, and small sandstone and limestone rock outcrops along the river. The trail is marked with 20 numbered posts corresponding to descriptions of the geology of the area, natural history, and human influence. The trail starts just west of the museum and descends down a set of wooden steps leading to the Rock River floodplain, parallels the river for a short distance, and then loops through a floodplain forest. An observation deck also overlooks the river.

Observation deck overlooking the Rock River, Black Hawk State Historic Site

REGULATIONS: Leash all pets. Groups of 25 or more must have a permit and must be supervised by 1 adult for each 15 minors. All vehicles must remain on roadway. No camping or ground fires permitted. No flowers, shrubs, trees, or other plants may be removed.

HOURS: The Hauberg Museum is open daily, 9:00 AM–12:00 PM and 1:00–5:00 PM, except Thanksgiving, Christmas, and New Year's Day. The site is open year-round, from sunrise to 10:00 PM.

DIRECTIONS: From I-280, turn north on US 67 (exit 15) and travel 1.3 miles to 46th Avenue. Turn east and travel 1 mile to the park. The parking lot and museum are on the south side of the road.

CONTACT INFORMATION: Black Hawk State Historic Site, 1510 46th Ave., Rock Island, IL 61201; (309) 788-0177; www.state.il.us/hpa/sites/blackhawk.htm

58.   Hidden Lakes Historic Trout Farm

HIGHLIGHTS:
- *Learning center with various displays and hands-on exhibits*
- *Staff naturalist*
- *DuPage River Greenway Bike Trail*
- *Fishing ponds and bait shop*
- *Interpretive signs around ponds*

PROGRAMS AND EVENTS:
- *Nature tours*
- *Family fun campfire*
- *Nature neighbors*
- *Trout fishing days*
- *Leaves and fall color*
- *Exploring the woods*

DESCRIPTION: Hidden Lakes Historic Trout Farm is a scenic, 15-acre park operated by the Bolingbrook Park District in Will County as a fishing and recreation area and an outdoor education resource. The site consists of 4 small lakes along the DuPage River as well as a bait shop and learning center. Along the shoreline of the lakes, willow trees drape their branches over the water. Also found here is the trailhead for the 1.5-mile, paved **DuPage River Greenway** bicycle/jogging trail. The learning center has a staff naturalist to conduct various tours and outdoor related programs. A seasonal catalog printed by the park district lists the programs offered throughout the year. Mowed grass paths and benches are scattered around the lakes, and 10 informational signs discuss the flora, fauna, and other items of general information.

REGULATIONS: No pets, campfires, tents, or alcoholic beverages permitted. Feeding of birds and other animals prohibited. Boats, canoes, rafts, and other flotation devices prohibited on the lakes. Charcoal grills allowed at south end of park only. No swimming, hunting, or trapping allowed. Check with bait shop for current fishing regulations. No driving on property.

HOURS: The grounds are open sunrise to sunset year-round. The learning center is open March–November, 10:00 AM–4:00 PM on Saturday; 11:00 AM–4:00 PM on Sunday.

Fishing and picnicking beside pond, Hidden Lakes Historic Trout Farm

DIRECTIONS: From I-55, go north on IL 53 (exit 267) for 2 miles to Boughton Road. Turn west and travel 1 mile to the entrance on the north side of Trout Farm Road and 2 more blocks to the parking area.

CONTACT INFORMATION: Hidden Lakes Historic Trout Farm, 425 Trout Farm Rd., Bolingbrook, IL 60440; (630) 759-8199

59. Isle a la Cache Museum

HIGHLIGHTS:
- *Museum with Native American and French exhibits*
- *80-acre island*
- *Interpreter*
- *Accessible trail and trail to the Des Plaines River*

PROGRAMS AND EVENTS:
- *Nature Tales*
- *Walk Through Time*
- *Cultural History Mystery*
- *When Two Worlds Meet*
- *Beaver Tracks and Trade*
- *To Build a Fire*
- *Native American Clay Crafts*
- *Native American Games*
- *Island Rendezvous*

DESCRIPTION: The Isle a la Cache Museum, operated by the Forest Preserve District of Will County on an 80-acre island surrounded by the Des Plaines River, is dedicated to the history of the French and Native American fur trade that was carried on in the region in the seventeenth

French exhibits, Isle a la Cache Museum

century. The name given to it by French-Canadians means "Island of the Hiding Place." Various exhibits on French and Native American culture include a video presentation and examples of canoes, animal skins, and a hut. Behind the museum is a short, paved, loop trail taking the visitor over a small bridge across a pond and to an amphitheater; a connecting trail goes over a boardwalk to the Des Plaines River. Another short trail heads east into the woods to some picnic tables and an access to another branch of the Des Plaines River. Half a mile east down 135th Street is the **Centennial Trail,** which leads north for 3 miles; there are plans to extend the trail south to Lockport.

REGULATIONS: Stay on trails.

HOURS: The museum is open Monday–Saturday, 10:00 AM–4:00 PM; Sunday, 12:00–4:00 PM.

DIRECTIONS: From I-55, head south on Weber Road (exit 263) for 1.2 miles to 135th Street. Turn east and go 3 miles, passing IL 53, and continue another .7 mile to the museum entrance on the south side of the road.

CONTACT INFORMATION: Isle a la Cache Museum, 501 E. Romeo Rd., Romeoville, IL 60446; (815) 886-1467; www.fpdwc.org

60. Illinois and Michigan Canal (Gaylord Donnelley Canal Trail)

HIGHLIGHTS:
- *Illinois and Michigan Canal National Heritage Corridor*
- *Gaylord Donnelley Building (a National Historic Landmark) housing the visitor center, exhibits, and Lockport Gallery Museum and Restaurant*
- *Pioneer settlement*
- *Interpretive trail*
- *Locks*
- *Illinois and Michigan Canal Museum*
- *Historic Lockport*

PROGRAMS AND EVENTS:
- *Pioneer settlement programs (e.g., Folk Art Festival, Journey into the Past, Pioneer Crafts Festival, Pioneer Christmas)*
- *Bike and Brake for History—guided bike tours*
- *Spring and summer dinner and lecture series*
- *The Canallers (period-dress interpreters)*
- *Trail walk*
- *Old Canal Day*

DESCRIPTION: The Illinois and Michigan (I&M) Canal, completed in 1848, stretched 96 miles, linking Lake Michigan with the Illinois River at LaSalle, and was used for 60 years before being abandoned when railroads and the Chicago Sanitary and Ship Canal were built. Today, the canal is open to various recreation uses, including a 2-mile stretch in Lockport (Will County) referred to as the **Lockport Historic Trail,** or the **Gaylord Donnelley Canal Trail.** The trail was named for the grandson of George Donnelley, who purchased the Gaylord Donnelley Building (the oldest building on the I&M Canal), which originally served as a warehouse for workers' supplies and then for grain storage. This trail has a paved and packed gravel surface, and it is a component of the 4.5-mile regional **Heritage Trail,** which extends from Lockport to the Joliet Iron Works Historic Site, and a component of the longer **Grand Illinois Trail.**

Next to the parking area is the Donnelley Building, which was restored in 1987 and contains the I&M Canal Visitor Center, the Illinois State Museum Lockport Gallery, and a restaurant. Directly south of the Gaylord Building is a pioneer settlement that the Will County Histori-

Pioneer settlement, Illinois and Michigan Canal (Gaylord Donnelley Canal Trail)

cal Society has restored. Pioneer buildings from Will County have been relocated here, and a herb garden, a well, a jail, and other buildings are on display along the canal. East of the pioneer settlement is the I&M Canal Museum, which originally served as headquarters for the canal.

The canal trail takes visitors along the canal past lock 1 and the Norton Building, a restored 1850s structure once used to store grain for loading onto barges. Glass-encased signs along the trail explain the history of the Donnelley Building, the canal, the Norton Building, and a turning basin. Lock 1 is well preserved and worth the .5-mile hike or bike ride, but be careful walking around it because there are some steep drops. Shortly past lock 1 is a trail spur leading over the railroad tracks to Dellwood Park, where travelers go under the road and an old dam may be seen. This ends the canal trail segment. Visitors can continue along the Heritage Trail, going past locks 2, 3, and 4 and the Joliet Iron Works Historic Site and into Joliet. State and local plans include linking the Gaylord Donnelley Canal Trail through Joliet to connect with the existing 60-mile **I&M Canal Trail** currently open.

REGULATIONS: Stay on trail. No swimming, rappelling, horseback riding, campfires, snowmobiles, metal detectors, littering, or alcohol permitted. Leash all pets.

HOURS: The trail is open daily, sunrise to sunset. The visitor center is open Wednesday–Sunday, 10:00 AM–5:00 PM.

DIRECTIONS: From I-55, turn south on IL 53 (exit 267) and travel 1.2 miles to the IL 53/Joliet Road junction. Turn right and proceed 5.4 miles to IL 7. Turn left, go over the Des Plaines River, the Sanitary and Ship Canal, and the I&M Canal; turn left at IL 171. Go 1 block to

8th Street and turn left to the Gaylord Donnelley Visitor Center parking lot.

CONTACT INFORMATION: Illinois Department of Natural Resources, I&M Canal Visitor Center, 200 W. 8th St., Lockport, IL 60441; (815) 838-4830; www.dnr.state.il.us/lands/education/interprt/i&m.htm

61.   Joliet Iron Works Historic Site

HIGHLIGHTS:
- *60-acre historic site*
- *Interpretive and accessible trail*
- *Connection with the Heritage Trail to Lockport*

DESCRIPTION: The Joliet Iron Works Historic Site in Will County is a fascinating historic location featuring various ruins and blast furnaces that produced steel from the 1870s to the 1930s. During that time, the plant employed over 3,000 workers, making Joliet one of the top steel producers in the world. Today, visitors get a chance to walk among these ruins on a 1.5-mile, paved trail with 10 interpretive signs detailing the story of steel production, the workers, and the production process. Tours of the site are also available. The trail starts as part of, and splits off from, the 4.5-mile **Heritage Trail,** which goes past locks 4, 3, and 2 of the Illinois and Michigan (I&M) Canal and continues on to Lockport, where it connects with the **Gaylord Donnelley Trail.**

REGULATIONS: No motorized vehicles allowed.

HOURS: The site is open only during daylight for safety.

Trail and interpretive signs, Joliet Iron Works Historic Site

97

DIRECTIONS: From I-80, go north on Chicago Street (exit 132B), which turns into Scott Street, for 2 miles to Columbia Street. Turn right and go 1 block to the parking lot entrance.

CONTACT INFORMATION: Forest Preserve District of Will County, 22606 S. Cherry Hill R., PO Box 1069, Joliet, IL 60434; (815) 727-8700; www.fpdwc.org

62. Pilcher Park Nature Center

HIGHLIGHTS:
- *Nature center with displays, live-animal exhibits (fish, turtles), and gifts*
- *Bird Haven Greenhouse and Conservatory*
- *Horticulture center*
- *Flowing well*
- Nature Journal *newsletter*
- *630-acre park*
- *Accessible and interpretive trails*

PROGRAMS AND EVENTS:
- *Academic Achievement Programs (e.g., Native American Lifestyles, Soil and Aquatic Adventures, Prickly Plants, Science, Snakes and Salamanders, Rainforest Adventures)*
- *Children's programs (Weather and Me, Rabbits and Bunnies, Leaf Out, Aquatic Adventures, Native American Work and Play, Pond Studies, Reptile/Amphibian Mania, Leaf and Tree Identification, Winter Tree Identification)*
- *Special events (e.g., Maple Sugaring, Wildflower Weekends, Quarterly Family Campfires, Halloween Hike, Changing of the Leaves Festival, Breakfast with Santa, Holiday Candle Walk, Fishing Contest, Syruping Demos, Earth Day Weekend, Winter-fest)*
- *Overnight programs*
- *Nature Journaling*
- *Stone Soup Day*
- *Sounds of the Forest Campfire*
- *Field trips*
- *Wednesday Walkers*
- *Winter Wonderland Nature Day*
- *Spring Crafts from Nature*

DESCRIPTION: Pilcher Park is a 630-acre park and nature center operated by the Joliet Park District in Will County. The park consists of a nature center and associated trails, the Bird Haven Greenhouse and Conservatory, the horticulture center, and a flowing water well. Hickory Creek flows through the park, and some fine fishing opportunities are available. The **Sensory Trail** (accessible), directly behind the nature center, is a .25-mile, paved trail with a rope that visitors can grab and follow,

*Nature center,
Pilcher Park
Nature Center*

which leads to a fountain and a small garden. The **Trail of Oaks** connects with the Sensory Trail and loops for .75 mile through a lowland oak forest. The **Walk in the Woods** is a .25-mile loop trail taking visitors past some interpretive markers. Additional trails in the park lead east towards the flowing well, Bird Haven, and the horticulture center.

REGULATIONS: Stay on trails.

HOURS: The park is open daily, 9:00 AM to sunset. The nature center is open 9:00 AM–4:30 PM in winter, and 9:00 AM–6:00 PM in summer. The horticulture center is open 9:00 AM–4:30 PM. The greenhouse is open 8:30 AM–4:30 PM.

DIRECTIONS: From I-80, head west on US 30 (exit 137) for 1 mile to Gouger Road. Turn north and go .5 mile to the park entrance. The nature center is 1 mile from Gouger Road.

CONTACT INFORMATION: Joliet Park District, 3000 W. Jefferson St., Joliet, IL 60435; (815) 741-7277; www.jolietpark.org/pilcher.htm

63.   Thorn Creek Nature Center

HIGHLIGHTS:
- *Historic church building*
- *Nature center with exhibits and programs*
- *Restored prairie*

PROGRAMS AND EVENTS:
- *Owl Prowls*
- *Native Remnants*
- *Winter Tracking and Trail Sense*
- *After school adventures*
- *Fall color walks*
- *Nature walk*

DESCRIPTION: The Thorn Creek Nature Center in Park Forest is housed in a historic church building surrounded by 850 acres of woodlands, wetlands, and prairie that are part of the Will County Forest Preserves. There are 2 loop trails, the .5-mile **Nature Center Trail** and the 1.25-mile **Upland Woodland Trail.** Also, the .75-mile (one-way) **Owl Lake Trail** is accessed at the west end of the Upland Woodland Trail. These trails have dirt and crushed rock surfaces. Within the preserve are many tree species, including sugar maple, elm, red oak, black walnut, and linden. Sumac and hawthorn are commonly seen along the Nature Center Trail. There is a long, narrow boardwalk passing through a shagbark hickory woodland area of the Upland Woodland Trail loop.

REGULATIONS: Remain on trails. Do not remove anything.

HOURS: The trails are open daily, 8:00 AM–8:00 PM. The nature center is open Thursday–Sunday, 12–4:00 PM; closed Thanksgiving, Christmas, and New Year's Day.

DIRECTIONS: From I-57 or I-94, take US 30 (the Lincoln Highway) to Western Avenue and head south to Steger-Monee Road. Follow it to the southwest, where it becomes Old Monee Road. The parking lot is on the east side of Old Monee Road, 2 miles southwest of the intersection of Western Avenue and Steger-Monee Road.

CONTACT INFORMATION: Thorn Creek Nature Center, 247 Monee Rd., Park Forest, IL 60466; (708) 747-6320

64.   Goodenow Grove Forest Preserve

HIGHLIGHTS:
- *Plum Creek Nature Center*
- *Accessible trail*

PROGRAMS AND EVENTS:
- *Early Learner's Exercise Trail*
- *Sniff, Look, Listen*
- *Everybody Needs a Rock*
- *Sights Unseen*
- *Taste of the Wild*
- *Stalking the Wild Tracks*
- *Whooo's Bones*
- *Bringing Up Baby*
- *Bugs, Bugs, Bugs!*
- *Nature Works Café*
- *Earth fair*

DESCRIPTION: Goodenow Grove Forest Preserve is 3 miles south of Crete in Will County. The short **Trail of Thoughts,** designed for people with disabilities, displays the diversity of the local flora and fauna. The trail begins south across the park road from the Plum Creek Nature Center. A trail board is visible at the trailhead, and other information sign boards are found along the way. The trail is a .25-mile loop with an asphalt surface. The other trails in the preserve offer another 4 miles of hiking, ranging from .5-mile to 1-mile connecting loops to the north of the nature center.

REGULATIONS: Permits required for camping.

HOURS: The nature center is open Tuesday–Saturday, 10:00 AM–4:00 PM; Sunday, 12–4:00 PM.

DIRECTIONS: Take IL 1 south from Crete to Goodenow Road, near the intersection of IL 1 and IL 394 (the Calumet Expressway). Turn east on Goodenow for 1.5 miles to the sign on Dutton Road leading north into the preserve.

CONTACT INFORMATION: Plum Creek Nature Center, Goodenow Grove Forest Preserve, 27604 Dutton Rd., Beecher, IL 60401; (708) 946-2216

65.   Goose Lake Prairie State Natural Area

HIGHLIGHTS:
- *Largest prairie remnant in Illinois*
- *1,537-acre Illinois Nature Preserve*
- *Interpretive center with slide show and exhibits on fish, other animals, and prairies*
- *130 bird species*
- *Accessible and interpretive trails*
- *Numerous wildflowers, prairie plants, birds, and other wildlife*
- *Log cabin*

PROGRAMS AND EVENTS:
- *Butterfly Gardens*
- *Backyard Bird Feeding*
- *Cabin Festival*
- *Hummingbirds Close Up*
- *Track and Tracking*
- *Call of the Wild*
- *Prairie Week Celebration*
- *Guided hikes*
- *Guided summer wagon tours*
- *Lectures*
- *Kids' fishing derby*

DESCRIPTION: Goose Lake Prairie State Natural Area in Grundy County is a rich biological area that contains 1,700 acres of prairie and marsh. Numerous wildflowers and animals may be seen in the park, and interpretive and hiking trails provide access to the prairie and marsh areas. The visitor center displays exhibits on the prairies and a slide show. The .5-mile **Marsh Loop Trail** loops past a small marsh and pond, and a boardwalk takes the visitor over the pond. It also connects with the **Tall Grass Nature Trail,** which begins behind the visitor center. This is an interpretive trail taking visitors through the heart of the largest grass prairie remnant left in the state. The trail is marked with 17 numbered stations that are described in a trail guide. A trail board, bench, and water fountain are at the start of the trail. Seen along the trail is the Craig Cabin, a reconstructed pioneer cabin, as well as a glacial pond. Be aware that this trail goes through open prairie, so there is no shade. The 3.5-mile **Prairie View Trail** is also available for hiking.

REGULATIONS: No camping or alcohol permitted. Leash pets. Do not feed wildlife. Stay on trails.

HOURS: The visitor center is open daily, 10:00 AM–4:00 PM. The park closes at sunset.

DIRECTIONS: From I-55, go west on Pine Bluff-Lorenzo Road (exit 240) for 7.2 miles to Jugtown Road. Turn north and follow the signs 1 mile to the visitor center on the east side of the road.

CONTACT INFORMATION: Goose Lake Prairie State Natural Area, 5010 N. Jugtown Rd., Morris, IL 60450; (815) 942-2849; www.dnr.state.il.us/lands/landmgt/parks/i&m/east/goose/home.htm

66.   Kankakee River State Park

HIGHLIGHTS:
- *Visitor center with exhibits and programs*
- *Rock Creek, canyon, and waterfall*
- *Scenic Kankakee River*
- *Upland forest*
- *Interpretive trail*
- *Chief Shawwawnasee grave site*
- *Wildflowers*

PROGRAMS AND EVENTS:
- *Children's programs*
- *Senior citizen programs*
- *Campground programs*
- *Guided hikes and walks*
- *Fall color walks*
- *Cross-country ski hikes*
- *Guided canoe trips*
- *Self-guided geology walks*
- *Theatiki—French and Indian War reenactment*
- *Kankakee River clean-up*

DESCRIPTION: Kankakee River State Park, in Kankakee County, is a beautiful linear park along the Kankakee River that offers numerous recreation opportunities, including camping, hiking, horseback riding, bike riding, canoeing, fishing, and exploring. A visitor center at the park entrance offers exhibits and various programs throughout the year, and there are numerous trails in the park. Two short, scenic interpretive trails are described here.

The **Chief Shawwawnasee Nature Trail,** 1.5 miles in length, parallels the clear, rock-lined Rock Creek, on the north side of IL 102. The trail is marked with 20 brown fiberglass posts corresponding to a trail brochure published by the park. This loop trail offers beautiful views of Rock Creek (first 11 posts), goes into an upland forest past wildflowers and a pond, and leads to the grave of Chief Shawwawnasee. A plaque on a large boulder describes how the last Potawatomi chief in this area was laid to rest there. A portion of this trail joins a horse trail; the numbered posts are useful markers as the trails join and split off from each other a few times. Wildlife abound in the area, including deer, wild turkey, and various bird species. Rock Creek is a good place to fish for smallmouth bass, and trout have also been introduced into the creek. Watch for spring wildflowers; and in the fall, the sumac colors are spectacular.

The **Rock Creek Trail,** leading through a wooded area towards Rock Creek Canyon and a waterfall, is .75-mile long and is part paved and part dirt. A 3-foot waterfall may be seen from the bluff top. The parking area and trailhead is on the north side of IL 102.

Please note: Steep cliffs, drop-offs, and other hazardous areas exist within the park. Please take proper precautions.

REGULATIONS: No swimming, camping, fires, alcohol, or motorized vehicles permitted. Leash all pets.

HOURS: The park closes at 10:00 PM. The visitor center is open Wednesday, Thursday, and Sunday, 8:00 AM–4:00 PM; Friday, 10:00 AM–6:00 PM; and Sunday, 12:00–8:00 PM. Hours may be different in the winter months.

DIRECTIONS: From I-57, go south on IL 50 (exit 315) for 1.5 miles to Armour Road. Turn west, travel a short distance to IL 102, and follow it west. The main park entrance and visitor center is a little over 6 miles, on the south side of the road. To reach the Chief Shawwawnasee Nature Trail, turn north at 5000 West Deselm Road and travel 1.3 miles to the trailhead on the west side of the road.

CONTACT INFORMATION: Kankakee River State Park, PO Box 37, Bourbonnais, IL 60914; (815) 933-1383; www.dnr.state.il.us/lands/landmgt/parks/r2/kankakee.htm

67.   Aroma Forest Preserve

HIGHLIGHTS:
- *Interpretive trail with 39 numbered stations*
- *6 different habitats*
- *Prairie restoration area*
- *Views of the Kankakee River*
- *Tall stand of red pines*
- *Upland/floodplain forest*

DESCRIPTION: Aroma Forest Preserve, east of Kankakee in Kankakee County, is a beautiful 55-acre park and home to a 2.2-mile interpretive trail that winds its way past some red pines, an oak-hickory forest, a restored prairie, wetlands, and a floodplain forest before ending at the Kankakee River. Wildflowers may be seen in the springtime, as well as numerous bird species and other wildlife; and flood conditions are possible along the lower part of the trail. Views of the river and Goat Island may be seen from the furthest point along the trail. The trail has 39 numbered metal posts corresponding to descriptions of the area in the preserve's trail guide.

REGULATIONS: No snowmobiling, camping, hunting, fires, motorized vehicles, or alcohol permitted. Leash all pets.

HOURS: The park is open daily, October–March, 6:00 AM–5:00 PM; and April–September, 6:00 AM–8:30 PM.

DIRECTIONS: From I-57, go east on IL 17 (exit 312) out of Kankakee and travel 4.5 miles to Hieland Road. Turn south and travel 1.5 miles to the parking area on the west side of the road.

CONTACT INFORMATION: Kankakee River Valley Forest Preserve District, 150 N. Schuyler Ave., 2nd Floor, Suite 1008, Kankakee, IL 60901; (815) 935-5630

Central Illinois

68. Humiston Woods Nature Center

HIGHLIGHTS:
- *300 acres of woods along the Vermilion River*
- *6 trails totaling over 6 miles (including an accessible trail)*
- *15-acre restored prairie*
- *Wildflowers*
- *Viewing platforms overlooking the Vermilion River*
- *Fishing pond*

PROGRAMS AND EVENTS:
- *School tours*

DESCRIPTION: Humiston Woods Nature Center is a beautiful wooded tract west of Pontiac (Livingston County) along the Vermilion River. Found here are over 30 tree species, abundant wildflowers, a restored prairie, a fishing pond, a canoe dock, picnic facilities, and shelters along with 6 trails totaling over 6 miles. A main trail board at the parking area along with a trail map enables the visitor to easily hike the trail network at this park. Operated by a nonprofit group, this "outdoor education" site is called a nature center, although there is no nature center building on the grounds. The trails wind between the Vermilion River and Wolf Creek through uplands and into the floodplain. The trails are all color coded and marked with unique symbols, such as a deer head for the **Deer Trail** or a mushroom for the **Mushroom Trail.** The **River Trail,** located to the left of the parking area, allows people with disabilities easy access to the **Fox Trail,** which is paved. Along the Fox Trail are a platform overlooking the river, a shelter, accessible rest rooms, a well, and benches.

REGULATIONS: No picking of flowers allowed. Do not litter.

HOURS: The site is open daily, 8:00 AM until dusk.

DIRECTIONS: From I-55, turn north on IL 23 (exit 201) and travel 1 mile to Rowe Road (2100N). Turn west and travel 3.8 miles until a sign and parking lot are seen on the north side of the road.

CONTACT INFORMATION: Humiston Woods Nature Center, PO Box 73, Pontiac, IL 61764

69.   Forest Park Nature Center

HIGHLIGHTS:
- *Interpretive center with displays, hands-on exhibits, multimedia computer station, and nature store*
- *540-acre park with a 454-acre Illinois Nature Preserve*
- *Over 7 miles of trails (including accessible and interpretive trails)*
- *Bird-feeding station*
- Tracks and Trails *newsletter*

PROGRAMS AND EVENTS:
- *Signs of Spring*
- *Early Worm Bird Walks*
- *Fall Tree ID*
- *Traveling naturalist*
- *Guided tours*
- *Field trips*
- *Birding for beginners*
- *Concert series*
- *Wildflower hikes*

DESCRIPTION: Forest Park Nature Center is a wooded and hilly 540-acre park and Illinois Nature Preserve in Peoria County, north of the city of Peoria along the bluffs of the Illinois River. The site features an A-frame interpretive center and nature bookstore, various exhibits and displays, year-round programs, and more than 7 miles of trails leading through an oak-hickory forest and a restored prairie. An excellent way to explore the site is by following the interpretive and accessible **Valley Trail** (1 mile) and **Valley Loop Trail** (.75 mile). Along these trails are 10 numbered posts corresponding to descriptions found in the pre-schooler's trail guide available at the center. These trails take the visitor along a wooded segment and a small creek and past a restored prairie. They also connect with other trail segments that lead up the hillside to the top of a bluff and some good views of the river valley. The Valley Trail is spectacular, with various wildlife such as squirrels and deer and various bird species.

REGULATIONS: No pets, bicyclists, or skiers allowed. No collecting of plants permitted. Dispose of litter properly. Stay on trails.

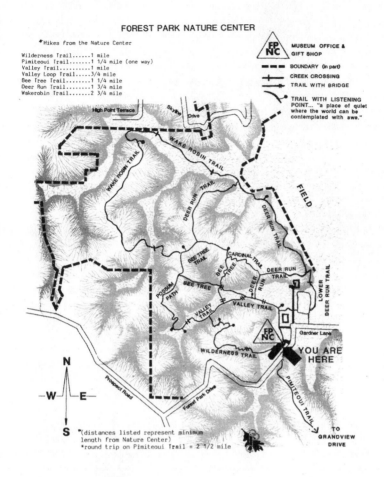

FOREST PARK NATURE CENTER

*Hikes from the Nature Center

Wilderness Trail......1 mile
Pimiteoui Trail.......1 1/4 mile (one way)
Valley Trail..........1 mile
Valley Loop Trail.....3/4 mile
Bee Tree Trail........1 1/4 mile
Deer Run Trail........1 3/4 mile
Wakerobin Trail.......2 3/4 mile

MUSEUM OFFICE &
GIFT SHOP

▬ ▬ ▬ BOUNDARY (in part)

CREEK CROSSING

TRAIL WITH BRIDGE

TRAIL WITH LISTENING
POINT... "a place of quiet
where the world can be
contemplated with awe."

*(distances listed represent minimum
length from Nature Center)
*round trip on Pimiteoui Trail = 2 1/2 mile

HOURS: The trails are open daily, dawn to dusk. The nature center and nature store are open Monday–Saturday, 9:00 AM–5:00 PM, and Sunday, 1:00–5:00 PM.

DIRECTIONS: From I-74, take IL 29 north out of Peoria for 5 miles to Gardner Lane, where a sign is seen for the nature center. Turn west on Gardner Lane and travel .6 mile to the parking area.

CONTACT INFORMATION: Forest Park Nature Center, 5809 Forest Park Dr., Peoria Heights, IL 61614; (309) 686-8820; www.peoriaparks.org

70. Hazel and Bill Rutherford Wildlife Prairie State Park

HIGHLIGHTS:

- *2,000-acre wildlife park with bison, elk, deer, bear, wolf, and other animals in a natural setting*
- *Wildlife viewing decks*
- *Visitor center with exhibits, gift shop, and orphan animal nursery*
- *Nature center*
- *Prairie Country Store*
- *Pioneer farmstead*
- *Butterfly garden and trail*
- *Restored prairie*
- *Lodging at Cabin on the Hill, Cottages by the Lake, Train Cabooses, Prairie Stables, and the Outback (accessible hotel rooms)*
- *Prairie railroad train rides*
- *Wildflowers*

PROGRAMS AND EVENTS:

- *Summer programs (e.g., Day Camps for Kids, Knee-High Naturalists, Night in the Wild, Starlight Walks)*
- *Naturalist programs*
- *Swing into Spring*
- *Giant Easter Egg Hunt*
- *Native American Powwow*
- *Wildlife Rendezvous*
- *Wildlife Scary Park*
- *Prairie parent (wildlife adoption)*
- *Breakfast on the prairie*
- *Rock and reptile show*
- *Teacher/educator workshops*
- *Leaf collecting workshop*
- *One wild winter day camp*

DESCRIPTION: Wildlife Prairie State Park, west of Peoria (Peoria County), consists of over 2,000 acres of rolling hills that were once mined for coal. Today, the area has been transformed into a zoo/wildlife preserve in a natural setting and is a sister park to the Brookfield Zoo in Chicago. It has been operated by the Forest Park Foundation since the

Pioneer farmstead, Hazel and Bill Rutherford Wildlife Prairie State Park

1960s and was purchased in 1999 by the State of Illinois. In 2001, the governor renamed the park in honor of Hazel and Bill Rutherford, founders of the park. The visitor center has displays on animals and a Native American gift shop as well as a viewing window on the wolf area. Various trails are located within the park; a few are described here. There is a general admission fee to the park.

Outside the visitor center, the **Butterfly Garden Trail** is a short trail that takes the visitor to a butterfly garden where various wildflowers are planted.

The Animal Trails (**Wagon Trail Loop, Merrill Woods Loop, Linder Trail,** and **Hellige Hiking Trail**) are located north of the visitor center and take the visitor past such animals as wolves, bobcats, bears, red foxes, gray foxes, and badgers and to a viewing deck overlooking black bears as well as the bison, elk, and deer pasture. The Wagon Trail Loop leads to a pioneer playground, with connecting trails leading to a pioneer farmstead and an old schoolhouse. The Hellige Hiking Trail leads to a waterfowl blind and an overlook of North Lake. Because it leads up a small hill, it is more difficult than the other animal trails.

The **Sliding Board Trail** starts west of the exhibition hall and takes the visitor to a 50-foot slide. A parking area is found to the west.

Other trails (**Whispering Hiking Trail, Hidden Lake Hiking Trail, Herbert B. White Hiking Trail**) are found near the train depot and take the visitor to a more remote part of the park that nature has reclaimed from previous mining activities. The trails lead the visitor past a few of the strip mine lakes and some wooded areas. Benches are found along the trails where there are some lake overlooks and large cottonwoods.

REGULATIONS: No pets, fire, or alcohol allowed. Stay on designated trails. Bicycles, skateboards, and roller blades are prohibited. No collecting of plant or animal specimens allowed.

HOURS: The park is open daily, 9:00 AM–4:30 PM, March–April and October–mid-December; 9:00 AM–6:30 PM, May–September.

DIRECTIONS: From I-474 west of Peoria, take the Farmington exit (exit 3A) and head west for 1.5 miles to Maxwell Road. Turn south and go .3 mile to IL 116. Turn west and go nearly 3 miles to Taylor Road. Turn north and go 3 miles to the park entrance on the east side of the road. From I-74, take exit 82 and travel south for 5 miles to the park entrance.

CONTACT INFORMATION: Hazel and Bill Rutherford Wildlife Prairie State Park, 3826 N. Taylor Rd., RR 2 Box 50, Peoria, IL 61615; (309) 676-0998; www.peoriatrader.com/wildlife/

71. Merwin Nature Preserve

HIGHLIGHTS:
- *Interpretive trail*
- *Upland and bottomland forests*
- *Spring wildflowers*
- *Mackinaw River, proposed as a Wild and Scenic River*
- *Suspension bridge*
- *Various outings and volunteer opportunities*
- *Savanna and prairie*

DESCRIPTION: Merwin Nature Preserve, near Bloomington in McLean County, is owned by the Parklands Foundation, a nonprofit organization dedicated to preserving open lands in McLean and Woodford counties in central Illinois. At 730 acres, Merwin is the largest tract owned by the foundation and is a beautiful forested property bisected by the Mackinaw River. Trails are on both sides of the river. An excellent way to explore the preserve is the 2-mile interpretive loop **Nature Trail** on the north side of the river; the trailhead may be found at the west gate. This dirt and wood-chip trail has 20 numbered posts correspond-

Suspension bridge over the Mackinaw River, Merwin Nature Preserve

ing to information presented in the Nature Trail Guide booklet and winds through upland and bottomland forests, along the bluff line of the Mackinaw River, and down to the river. Good views of the Mackinaw River may be had along the trail, and in April and May many wildflowers bloom, including trillium, Jacob's ladder, bloodroot, and bluebells, to name a few. A suspension bridge takes visitors to the south side of the preserve, where the **Elizabeth Stein Trail** and **Henline Woods Trail** may be hiked to County Highway 8. The Nature Trail continues paralleling the river for a short distance, parallels and then crosses a small creek, and winds through an upland oak forest.

REGULATIONS: Pets, bicycles, and motorized vehicles prohibited.

HOURS: The preserve is open during daylight hours.

DIRECTIONS: From I-55, take the Lexington exit (exit 178) and head west on County Highway 8 (2500N) for 5 miles to Gridley Road. Turn north and proceed .6 mile, crossing the Mackinaw River. A small parking lot is on the east side of the road.

CONTACT INFORMATION: Parklands Foundation, PO Box 3132, Bloomington, IL 61702-3132; www.parklands.org

72.   Comlara Park

HIGHLIGHTS:
- *Visitor center with exhibits and wildlife displays*
- *Campground*
- *925-acre Evergreen Lake*
- *3 interpretive trails plus other hiking and mountain biking trails*
- *Swimming beach*
- *175 bird species*

PROGRAMS AND EVENTS:
- *Nature walks*

DESCRIPTION: Comlara Park at Evergreen Lake is a public recreation complex operated by the McLean County Parks and Recreation Department. Evergreen Lake is the water reservoir for the cities of Bloomington and Normal. There is no commercial development around the lake except for recreation facilities, which include a campground and a swimming beach. A visitor center at the park entrance has rest rooms and a staff naturalist on hand, along with various animal and Native American displays, park brochures, trail guides, and other information. Numerous trails wind their way around the lake, including 10 miles of hiking and mountain biking trails as well as 3 interpretive trails that are described here.

The **Self-Guided Interpretive Trail** is a 1,000-foot, packed gravel (accessible) trail that begins outside the visitor center. This trail has 13 marked stations corresponding to descriptions in an associated brochure of the various trees found along the trail. The trail ends at the service road; the **Deer Island Trail** picks up on the other side of the service road.

The **Hickory Grove Nature Trail** starts directly across the street from the visitor center, at the trailhead in the campground entrance parking area. The trail is .12 mile along a gravel surface and features 13 numbered posts corresponding to various descriptions in the park brochure. At the trailhead are a trail sign and a mailbox with maps. The trail loops around a small wooded area and goes by Evergreen Lake and a small picnic area with tables, grills, and trash cans. A dirt path leads down to the lake, where a drop-off is encountered; be careful at this spot, particularly with children.

Family outing along self-guided interpretive trail, Comlara Park

The **Shady Hollow Nature Trail,** at the south end of the lake along Six Mile Creek, may be reached by car or by a 2.5- to 3-mile hike or bike ride. This .5-mile, interpretive trail has 13 numbered posts corresponding to descriptions in an associated brochure. The trail winds through uplands, by a small prairie, and down to the floodplain of Six Mile Creek. The trail was originally developed in the 1970s as a loop; when the lake level was raised and the lower trail surface became inundated, the trail was shortened and became one-way. As this trail is less traveled, numerous bird and animal species may be seen along its path.

REGULATIONS: Alcoholic beverages and gathering of firewood prohibited. No parking on grass. Swimming in Evergreen Lake is prohibited except at designated beach area. Leash all pets. There is a 10-horsepower limit on the lake, and a watercraft registration is required. Stay on trails.

HOURS: The park closes at 10:00 PM.

DIRECTIONS: From I-39, head west on Lake Bloomington Road (exit 8) for 1.4 miles to McLean County Road 33, where a sign for Comlara Park may be seen. Turn left and head 1.1 miles to the park entrance on the right side of the road.

CONTACT INFORMATION: Comlara Park, Department of Parks and Recreation, RR 1 Box 73, Hudson, IL 61746; (309) 726-2022

73.   Moraine View State Park

HIGHLIGHTS:
- *1,678-acre site*
- *The Bloomington Moraine*
- *Upland landscape*
- *158-acre lake*
- *Interpretive and accessible trails*
- *Controlled pheasant hunting*

DESCRIPTION: Moraine View State Park is a wooded, upland park found on the Bloomington Moraine (glacial deposit) in McLean County. At this scenic park is the 158-acre Dawson Lake, as well as the typical picnic and camping facilities found at most state parks. In the fall, the park office keeps numerous pheasants in wire cages before releasing them in the park for a controlled hunt. Three trails are at Moraine View State Park, 2 of which are described here. The **Tanglewood Nature Trail** is a .5-mile, interpretive loop that starts just past the park office. The trail has 13 fiberglass numbered posts corresponding to a descriptions in the associated trail brochure of the plants, animals, and geology of the area. Along the trail are benches, viewing platforms, and a boardwalk. The trail winds through a small woodland down to a marsh and a restored prairie. As the area is near a controlled pheasant hunting area, pheasants are occasionally seen along or near the trail. The **Timber Point Accessible Trail** is a .25-mile, paved loop near Dawson Lake. A wooded peninsula makes this a scenic trail, and great blue herons and other bird species are sometimes seen along the lake.

REGULATIONS: Do not litter. No open fires allowed. Leash pets. There is a 10-horsepower limit on Dawson Lake. No fishing permitted in creek below the dam.

HOURS: The park closes at 10:00 PM. The office is open daily, 8:00 AM– 3:30 PM.

DIRECTIONS: From I-74 east of Bloomington, turn north at exit 149 for LeRoy. Follow US 150 west to West Street (County Road 21). Fol-

TANGLEWOOD NATURE TRAIL MAP

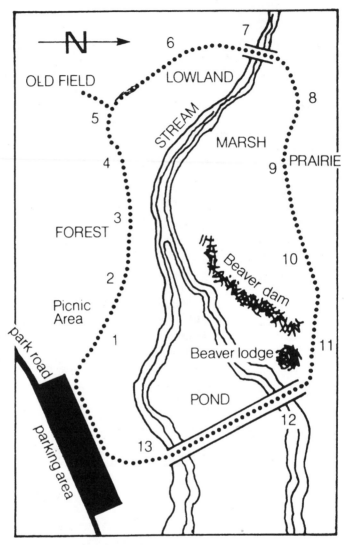

Hiking Difficulty: Slight   Length ½ mile

low it north for 4 miles to 875N. Turn east and travel 1.3 miles to the park entrance.

CONTACT INFORMATION: Moraine View State Park, RR 2, LeRoy, IL 61752; (309) 724-8032; www.dnr.state.il.us/lands/landmgt/parks/r3/moraine.htm

74. Nauvoo Historic Site

HIGHLIGHTS:
- *Visitor center with numerous exhibits, documents, and audiovisual presentations*
- *Joseph Smith Historic Center*
- *Over 30 restored homes*
- *Trail of Hope interpretive trail*
- *Sculpture garden*
- *Horse and carriage rides*
- *Site listed on the National Register of Historic Places*

PROGRAMS AND EVENTS:
- *Pioneer Pastimes*
- *City of Joseph Pageant*
- *Sunset by the Mississippi campfire*
- *Musical dramas about old Nauvoo*
- *Hands-on activities at the brickyard and Coolidge home*

DESCRIPTION: Nauvoo Historic Site in Hancock County, home to Joseph Smith and his Mormon followers from 1839 to 1846, features over 30 restored sites and buildings, the Mississippi River to the west, Nauvoo State Park across the street, and the historic town of Nauvoo. A good starting point is the visitor center, at the north end of the grounds, which has exhibits, documents, and an audiovisual presentation and offers a horse and carriage ride. The entire grounds may be toured by car or by carriage, and there are walking tours of the old village area. The .25-mile, interpretive **Trail of Hope** parallels the road from the Seventies Hall Building down to the Mississippi River. Along the trail are various signs quoting the pioneers who left Nauvoo in the mass exodus to lands west in 1846. Across the Mississippi River is the start of the **Mormon Pioneer National Historic Trail** that continues on to Salt Lake City. Also seen near the river is a pioneer memorial in honor of the 11,000 or so people who journeyed out of Nauvoo. In Nauvoo itself is the site of the old Nauvoo temple, which was burned in a fire and then leveled by a tornado and which is in the process of being rebuilt.

HOURS: The visitor center is open Monday–Saturday, 9:00 AM–5:00 PM, and Sunday, 1:00–5:00 PM.

DIRECTIONS: From US 136 west of Macomb, turn north on IL 96 and continue for 11 miles into Nauvoo. Follow the signs to the visitor cen-

*Calvin Pendle-
ton log home
and school,
Nauvoo
Historic Site*

ter. To reach the Trail of Hope, turn west on Parley Road, travel to the
Seventies Hall Building, and park where a sign is seen for the trail.

CONTACT INFORMATION: Nauvoo Restoration, Inc., Young and
Main Street, PO Box 215, Nauvoo, IL 62354; 1-888-453-6434;
www.visitnauvoo.org

75.   Lakeview Nature Center

HIGHLIGHTS:
- *350-acre site*
- *55-acre restored prairie*
- *Wetlands*
- *Nature center with various hands-on exhibits, displays, and programs*
- *Access to Spring Lake Park*

PROGRAMS AND EVENTS:
- *Prairie Exploration*
- *Moonlight Walk*
- *Saturday nature identification hikes*

DESCRIPTION: Lakeview Nature Center in McDonough County, open since 1998, is next to Spring Lake Park, just north of Macomb and the campus of Western Illinois University. It features year-round programs, interactive hands-on displays, and a staff naturalist on hand to act as guide or to participate in an activity. The nature center itself is built of hand-hewn oak timbers. Mowed grass paths wind their way through the restored prairies and wetlands at the site, and trails lead north towards Spring Lake Park, an additional 700 acres with a campground, picnic tables, rest rooms, showers, shelters, playground equipment, a concession stand (seasonal), and other hiking trails.

REGULATIONS: No motorized vehicles allowed on trails. Stay on trails. Ground fires, alcoholic beverages, firearms, swimming, and littering prohibited. Leash all pets.

HOURS: The nature center is open Wednesday and Friday, 12:00–6:00 PM; Saturday, 10:00 AM–6:00 PM; and Sunday, 1:00–6:00 PM.

DIRECTIONS: From US 67, go north out of Macomb for 1.5 miles to Spring Lake Road. Turn west and travel 2 miles until a sign is seen for the nature center along the north side of the road.

CONTACT INFORMATION: Lakeview Nature Center, 10050 N. 1500th Rd., Macomb, IL 61455; (309) 836-2887; TTY (309) 837-7301; www.macomb.com/~parks

76.   Emiquon National Wildlife Refuge

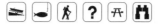

HIGHLIGHTS:
- *Wildlife viewing platform*
- *Numerous bird species*

DESCRIPTION: The Emiquon National Wildlife Refuge, a component of the Illinois River National Wildlife and Fish Refuges, is west of Havana in Fulton County. The **Frank C. Bellrose Nature Trail,** named in honor of a noted waterfowl scientist from Illinois, is a 1-mile loop atop a berm and along an old roadbed circling a low marshy area that attracts numerous birds and other animals. At the northern end, the trail parallels the Spoon River for a short distance, where there is an observation deck with benches for wildlife viewing. Bird species that may be seen here include osprey, turkey vulture, least sandpiper, kestrel, red-tailed hawk, northern pintail, great egret, and others; a trail board lists many of the species found at the site. There is a boat launch for the Spoon River at the north parking area. A wooden trail boardwalk parallels IL 78/97. Early spring through late fall is a good time to explore the nature trail, although the area may get inundated at times.

REGULATIONS: Off-road vehicle use is prohibited. Fires, overnight use, and camping not permitted. Nut, berry, and mushroom picking are allowed in areas open to the public during daylight hours.

HOURS: The refuge is open daily, sunrise to sunset.

DIRECTIONS: From Havana, take IL 78/97 west over the Illinois River for .75 mile past the bridge, then follow IL 78/97 north for .25 mile to the first small parking area; or continue another .25 mile to the north parking area for the Spoon River Public Access Area. Both parking areas are on the east side of the road.

CONTACT INFORMATION: Emiquon National Wildlife Refuge, Illinois River National Wildlife and Fish Refuges, 19031 E. County Rd. 2105N, Havana, IL 62644; (309) 535-2290; midwest.fws.gov/illinoisriver/emq.html

77.   Chautauqua National Wildlife Refuge

HIGHLIGHTS:
- *Refuge headquarters*
- *Accessible and interpretive trail*
- *Major bird-watching area*
- *3 scenic overlooks on Lake Chautauqua,*
  1 with accessible binoculars
- *Small prairie*

DESCRIPTION: The Chautauqua National Wildlife Refuge, along Lake Chautauqua, west of Buzzville and north of Havana in Mason County, is 1 of the 4 units that comprise the Illinois River National Wildlife and Fish Refuges (the others are Cameron-Billsbach, Meredosia, and Emiquon) totaling over 10,000 acres along a 124-mile stretch of the Illinois River in central Illinois. The Chautauqua refuge is 4,488 acres in size and home to numerous bird species; in fact, over 250 species have been recorded here. The .5-mile, accessible, interpretive **Chautauqua Nature Trail** (packed gravel surface) begins at the refuge headquarters. The trail is marked with 8 numbered posts that correspond to descriptions in the trail brochure available at the trailhead. The trail winds through upland and bottomland forest, paralleling the lake where there are 3 observation decks, 1 with a set of accessible binoculars. Various bird species that may be seen include great blue heron, bald eagle, owl, wood duck, great egret, and tundra swan. A bird checklist booklet is available from the US Fish and Wildlife Service office.

REGULATIONS: All activities are day-use only. No fires, overnight use, camping, or alcohol are permitted on the refuge. Nut, berry, and mushroom picking are allowed in areas open to the public during daylight hours.

HOURS: The nature trail is open daily, sunrise to sunset; refuge gate is locked at sunset. The refuge headquarters is open Monday–Friday, 8:00 AM–4:30 PM.

DIRECTIONS: Follow US 136 east out of Havana for 5 miles to 2130E. Turn north and go 3.5 miles to 2000N. Turn left and go nearly 2 miles to 1950E. Follow it a short distance until a sign is seen for the Illinois River National Wildlife Refuges, at 2110N. Turn west (left) and proceed .5 mile to the parking area at the refuge headquarters.

CONTACT INFORMATION: Chautauqua National Wildlife Refuge, Illinois River National Wildlife and Fish Refuges, 19031 E. County Rd., Havana, IL 62644; (309) 535-2290; midwest.fws.gov/illinoisriver/chaq.html

78.   Kickapoo Creek Park

HIGHLIGHTS:
- *160-acre wildlife park*
- *Floodplain forest*
- *12-acre restored prairie*
- *Wildflowers*
- *Birds and other wildlife*

DESCRIPTION: Kickapoo Creek Park, a 160-acre wildlife park in Lincoln, is operated by the Logan County Park and Trails Foundation, a nonprofit organization dedicated to the acquisition and preservation of properties in the county for the use and enjoyment of residents. The park is in a beautiful floodplain forest along Kickapoo Creek and features shelters, tables, grills, 3 miles of trails, a fitness trail, a Scout camp, and a restored prairie. The trail system consists of 1 mile of loop trails on the north side of the creek reached by means of a footbridge, and 2 miles of trails on the south side that lead to a few playground and picnic areas. On the south side, near the park entrance, a set of trails (**Route 66 Trail** and **Scully Trail**) wind around and through a restored prairie where wildflowers and wildlife thrive.

Red-winged blackbird in prairie, Kickapoo Creek Park

REGULATIONS: No alcohol, swimming, or dirt bikes permitted.

HOURS: The park is open daily, 7:00 AM to 1 hour after sunset.

DIRECTIONS: From I-55 northbound, head east on IL 10/121 (exit 126) for 1.9 miles to Lincoln Parkway. Turn left and travel .7 mile to the park entrance on the left. From I-55 southbound, exit at Business Route 55 (exit 133) and proceed 4.3 miles to the entrance on the right side of the road.

CONTACT INFORMATION: Kickapoo Creek Park, 2000 N. Jefferson St., Lincoln, IL 62656; (217) 735-2953

79. Weldon Springs State Recreation Area

HIGHLIGHTS:

- *Union School (1865) interpretive center with various displays and hands-on exhibits*
- *Prairie and wildflower garden*
- *Twin Springs and Old Faithful natural springs*
- *Interpretive trails*
- *425-acre park with various recreation opportunities*
- *29-acre fishing and boating lake*
- *Concession stand with boat rentals (seasonal)*
- *Wildlife carving*

PROGRAMS AND EVENTS:

- *School programs*
- *Eco-watch programs*
- *Campground naturalist programs on weekends*
- *Children's fishing derby*

DESCRIPTION: Weldon Springs State Recreation Area near Clinton in De Witt County has a 29-acre fishing and boating lake, nature/interpretive and backpacking trails, an interpretive center, a campground, picnic sites, natural springs, amphitheaters, and a concession stand (seasonal). The woodlands consist of a scenic oak-hickory forest along Weldon Springs Lake. From 1901 to 1921, the area was the site of annual chautauquas, where speakers held forth on a variety of topics in religion, education, and entertainment. Two natural springs (Old Faithful and Twin Springs) near the concession stand still have a small water flow from an old river known as the Teays. The old Union School and the Town Hall building at the south end of the park feature various displays, hands-on exhibits, and an old schoolroom. A staff naturalist, who works out of the Town Hall building, is on hand to discuss nature-related topics. During the summer months, the naturalist walks through the campground talking with campers.

The **Lakeside Self-Guided Nature Trail** circles the entire lake for 2 miles. The trailhead may be found to the east of the concession stand, where a bridge and a trail board are seen. Numerous other access points to the trail are throughout the park. The trail has 23 numbered posts that correspond to descriptions in the trail brochure. There are benches, rest rooms, and excellent views of the lake along the trail, as well as some wooded areas with oaks and hickories. Also found along the trail is

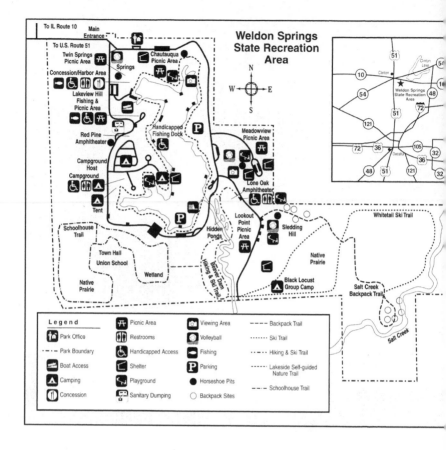

jewelweed, which attracts numerous hummingbirds in September, and a wildlife sculpture that was carved out of a dead bald cypress tree with a chainsaw. There are some steep climbs and wooden stairs along the trail; otherwise, the surface consists of dirt, gravel, concrete, and wood chips. Bring along your fishing pole and try your luck while hiking this trail. An accessible fishing dock is located off the trail.

The **Schoolhouse Trail** is in the Union School area (where a portion of the trail becomes a loop of the **Bluebird Trail**). The 1.3-mile trail loops around a restored prairie and the edge of a wooded area, goes past a small pond, and connects with the Beaver Dam Trail on the east. Numerous butterflies, wildflowers, and prairie grasses are seen throughout the summer months. Also, stop in the old Town Hall building to see an exhibit or talk with the staff naturalist.

The **Beaver Dam Trail** is a .8-mile wooded trail that may be reached near the Lone Oak Amphitheater, near the dam, from a ski trail, or from the Schoolhouse Trail. The trail winds down a wooded hillside, past a few ponds, parallels and then crosses a creek, then loops around, splits, and rejoins again at the creek. An unmarked spur trail leads uphill to the Schoolhouse Trail, along the west side of the loop. There are interpretive signs and a bench on the trail.

Other trails include the 1-mile **Salt Creek Trail,** a backpack trail that leads to Salt Creek and camping sites, and the 2.8-mile **Whitetail Ski Trail** that takes skiers into the Salt Creek floodplain, connecting with the backpacking trail and the Beaver Dam Trail.

HOURS: The interpretive center is open 8:30 AM–4:30 PM, Monday–Friday, Labor Day to Memorial Day, and Wednesday–Sunday, Memorial Day to Labor Day. Trails are open 6 AM–10:00 PM.

DIRECTIONS: From US 51, take Business Route 51 heading towards Clinton and turn east on 950E. Follow it 1 mile to 520N. Turn south and proceed 1.1 miles, following the signs to the park entrance.

CONTACT INFORMATION: Weldon Springs State Recreation Area, RR 2 PO Box 87, Clinton, IL 61727; (217) 935-2644; staff interpreter (217) 935-0373 www.dnr.state.il.us/lands/landmgt/parks/r3/weldonra.htm

80. Valentine Park

HIGHLIGHTS:
- *Nature trail with tree identification signs*
- *Bird-watching area*

DESCRIPTION: Valentine Park is a small and scenic wooded site on the outskirts of Monticello in Piatt County named in honor of Katherine Valentine, a teacher from Monticello who donated the land for the park; a plaque describes her contribution. A .5-mile, dirt and grass surfaced, nature and bird-watching loop trail features 15 tree markers identifying the species, which include sugar maple, wild cherry, honey locust, black walnut, oak, shagbark hickory, box elm, and hackberry. The trail loops through the woods past a bench and a wooden deck overlooking the bluff line. Be careful at this overlook; there is no rail.

REGULATIONS: Stay on designated trail.

HOURS: The park is open only during daylight for safety.

DIRECTIONS: From I-72 near Monticello, take the Bridge Street exit (exit 164). Turn east and go 1.2 miles to Market Street/IL 105. Turn north on IL 105 to 1730N, turn east, and go .6 mile to the park entrance on the north side of the road.

CONTACT INFORMATION: Piatt County Forest Preserve District, 700 N. Macon St., Bement, IL 61813-1008; (217) 762-4531

81.   Robert Allerton Park

- *1,500-acre site*
- *1,000-acre National Natural Landmark*
- *50-acre restored prairie*
- *Savanna*
- *Interpretive trail*
- *1,000 species of plants; 60 species of breeding birds; 30 species of mammals; 28 species of amphibians and reptiles*
- *Floodplain and upland forest*
- *Wildflowers*

DESCRIPTION: Allerton Park is near Monticello along the Sangamon River in Piatt County. On the north side of the river are the visitor center (with rest rooms, concessions, exhibits, gifts, water, and telephone), a conference center, flower gardens, sculptures, and the main trails. Various programs, classes, and lectures are offered at the park throughout the year.

The **Buck Schroth Interpretive Trail** is 1.5 to 3 miles long, depending on the loops hiked. The trail is named in honor of Eugene "Buck" Schroth, a teacher, self-taught naturalist, and former director of Allerton Park who also volunteered and led naturalist hikes. Along the **Southern Prairie Loop** on the south side of the river are 10 signs describing the prairies and the local flora and fauna, such as wildflowers, butterflies and other insects, mammals, and birds. A 50-acre restored prairie and a savanna are encountered as the trail winds through a floodplain forest and parallels the river for a short distance. Near the river, the trail joins the **Northern River Loop,** a 2-mile loop around the grounds that connects with nearly 10 miles of trails on the south side of the park.

REGULATIONS: No picking of any flowers, leaves, seeds, or fruits allowed. Stay on designated trails. Bicycles, horseback riding, and motorized vehicles restricted to roads only. Leash pets. No fishing, hunting, swimming, alcohol, open fires, or firearms are permitted.

HOURS: The park grounds are open daily, 8:00 AM until sunset. The visitor center is open daily, 8:00 AM–5:00 PM.

DIRECTIONS: From I-72 eastbound, go south on IL 48 (exit 156) for .2 mile to the frontage road (1525N). Turn east (left) on the frontage

Bird-watching on Buck Schroth Interpretive Trail, Robert Allerton Park

road and travel 6.5 miles to 625E, where a sign is seen for Allerton Park. From I-72 westbound, go south at the Monticello/IL 105 exit (exit 164) to IL 47. Turn west and proceed a few miles to 625E. Turn south and go about 1 mile to 1550N, turn west, and go .5 mile to Allerton Park Road. Turn south and follow this road for .8 mile to a stop sign. Traveling straight will take you to the conference center and visitor center. The Buck Schroth Trail is reached by turning left and following this road for 1.2 miles to the parking area on the right, just after crossing the Sangamon River.

CONTACT INFORMATION: Robert Allerton Park, 515 Old Timber Rd., Monticello, IL 61856; (217) 244-9982; www.ceps.uiuc.edu

82.   Lake of the Woods County Park

HIGHLIGHTS:
- *Early American Museum*
- *Botanical gardens*
- *Hi-tower bell carillon and observation area*
- *1892 town hall*
- *Covered bridge over Sangamon River*
- *Lake of the Woods*
- *900-acre preserve; 260 acres of prairie*

PROGRAMS AND EVENTS:
- *Earth's Natural Cycles*
- *Discovery Days for Children*
- *Morning Bird Walk*
- *Tree Identification*
- *A Picturesque Prairie*
- *Sights and Sounds of Summer*
- *Bug Basics*
- *Tricky Tracks*
- *Soil Sleuth*
- *What's in the Water?*
- *Freedom Fest*

DESCRIPTION: The Lake of the Woods County Park, northwest of Champaign, is operated by the Forest Preserve District of Champaign County. The site includes the Early American Museum, the forest preserve headquarters, Lake of the Woods, picnic facilities, a golf course, botanical gardens, a prairie, and a .5-mile loop nature trail. The trail is located in the Rayburn-Purnell Woods, an oak-hickory tract just southeast of the museum, and there is a trail board at the trailhead. In addition, the park features a 3.5-mile, paved bicycle trail as well as mowed grass paths in the prairie area on the west side of IL 47, just south of the museum. There is an admission fee to the museum.

REGULATIONS: Stay on trails.

HOURS: The park is open daily, 7:00 AM–8:00 PM. The Early American Museum is open daily, 10:00 AM–5:00 PM, between Memorial Day and Labor Day.

DIRECTIONS: From I-74, go north on IL 47 (exit 172) for .7 mile to the park entrance on the east side of the road.

CONTACT INFORMATION: Lake of the Woods County Park, PO Box 1040, Mahomet, IL 61853; (217) 586-3360; www.ccfpd.org/lowpark.htm

83. Anita Purves Nature Center and Busey Woods

- *Nature center with various exhibits, observation room, nature store, and education room*
- *Wildflower and butterfly gardens*
- *2.5 miles of trails in Busey Woods*
- Nature Watch *newsletter*
- Educational Services *brochure*
- *Bird-watching opportunities*

PROGRAMS AND EVENTS:

- *Preschool to sixth grade nature programs*
- *Seasonal programs (e.g., I'm a Nut, Bird Walks, Color Me Fall, Tracks)*

DESCRIPTION: The Anita Purves Nature Center in Urbana (Champaign County) is named in honor of a volunteer who led nature awareness walks with children and worked to build the nature center. Next to the nature center is the 59-acre Busey Woods, which was once part of a 10-square-mile Big Game Wooded Area consisting of forest and prairie. In the 1970s, the Busey Woods was purchased and preserved from commercial development. Within this area is a 2.5-mile trail system with various loops that take the visitor over the Saline Drainage Ditch (via a suspension bridge) and onto the wooded property where there are old oxbow lakes formed by the river prior to its channelization, a boardwalk, a hardwood forest, a successional area, and a small pond with an observation deck. Over 30 species of trees are located in this tract, and numerous spring woodland wildflowers and birds may be seen along the trail.

REGULATIONS: No littering, camping, hunting, trapping, or collecting of materials allowed. No motorized vehicles, pets, horses, picnics, or campfires permitted. Hike on designated trails only.

HOURS: The nature center is open September–May, Monday–Saturday, 8:00 AM–5:00 PM, and Sunday, 12:00–4:00 PM; June–August, Monday–Saturday, 8:00 AM–6:00 PM, and Sunday, 12:00–4:00 PM.

DIRECTIONS: From I-74, turn south on Cunningham Avenue (exit 184) in Urbana and go .7 mile to Country Club Road. Turn west

*Suspension
bridge leading
into woods,
Anita Purves
Nature Center
and Busey
Woods*

and go .4 mile to Broadway. Turn south and go 2 blocks to the parking lot.

CONTACT INFORMATION: Anita Purves Nature Center, 1505 N. Broadway, Urbana, IL 61801; (217) 384-4062; www.prairienet.org/upd/anitapurvesnaturecenter.html

84.   Meadowbrook Park

HIGHLIGHTS:
- *Restored prairie*
- *Sculpture garden*
- *Farm buildings and herb garden*
- *Wildflower and accessible trail*
- *Prairie playground*
- *Organic gardens*

DESCRIPTION: Meadowbrook Park, operated by the Urbana Park District (Champaign County) near the University of Illinois at Urbana-Champaign, features a restored prairie, a sculpture garden, a farm, gardens, a wildflower trail, and a paved bicycle path around the park. The restored prairie and associated paths are on the south side of the park, south of the creek, while the sculpture garden and the farm are on the north side. From the farm, the paved (accessible) **Peg Richardson Hickman Wildflower Trail** heads east for .25 mile, passing by planted beds of wildflowers and connecting with the paved trail around the sculpture garden, where sculptures and informational signs may be seen. Connecting trails and wooden bridges lead over the creek to dirt paths through the restored tallgrass prairie. Shelters, picnic tables, rest rooms, and water are near the farm and at the parking area off Windsor Road.

REGULATIONS: Stay on trails. Bicyclists, roller bladers, and skateboarders should stay on paved paths only. Leash dogs. No removal of park property or natural materials permitted.

HOURS: The park is open daily, dawn to dusk.

DIRECTIONS: From I-74, head south on Lincoln Avenue (exit 183) for 3.6 miles to Windsor Road. Turn east and go to Race Street. Turn south and go 2 blocks to reach the parking area for the farm. To reach the prairie playground area, continue on Windsor another 4 blocks past Race.

CONTACT INFORMATION: Urbana Park District, 303 W. University, Urbana, IL 61801; (217) 367-1536; www.prairienet.org/upd/meadowbrookpark.html

85.   Salt Fork River Forest Preserve

HIGHLIGHTS:

- *Environmental education center with various exhibits and displays (birds, animals, fish, butterflies, turtles)*
- *798-acre park*
- *80-acre lake*
- *Restored prairies*
- *Wildflowers*
- *Historic Maple Grove*
- *Accessible trail*
- *Observation platform*

PROGRAMS AND EVENTS:

- *Environmental education (e.g., Discovery Hikes, Sights and Sounds of Nature, Aquatic Awareness, Wetlands and Waterfowl, Prairie Patterns, Branching Out with Trees, Earth Keepers)*
- *Special programs (e.g., Geology of the Salt Fork River; Star Light, Star Bright, Let's Learn Stars; Owl Prowl)*
- *Tree Identification*
- *Earth's Natural Cycles*
- *What's in the Water?*
- *Tales of Adventure in Nature*
- *Naturalist in the Classroom*
- *Photographic Nature*

DESCRIPTION: Salt Fork Forest Preserve is a 798-acre recreation and wildlife tract owned and operated by the Champaign County Forest Preserve District. An 80-acre lake offers boating, fishing, and bird-watching, while the visitor center has many exhibits, general park information, various programs, and a staff naturalist. Shelters, picnic tables, and playgrounds are also available. Over 10 miles of hiking trails are located within the park, including an accessible trail leading to a wildlife viewing platform overlooking a restored prairie. Two of the trails are described here.

The **Timberdoodle Trail** is a 1.2-mile, partly accessible, loop trail starting at the visitor center and heading north. The first part of the trail is paved and leads to a restored prairie, where there is an observation tower for viewing the prairie and the wildlife in the area. Grass paths lead away from the tower into a successional wooded area, paralleling the lake, with some trail spurs leading down to the lake. One trail spur leads to the parking area northwest of the visitor center, where a short walk through an open field leads to the **Maple Sugar Grove Trail.** This is a .5-mile loop through the historic Maple Grove area where maple syrup was produced for many years. Towering sugar maples may be seen along this short trail, and interpretive signs along the trail describe the maple grove and other natural features of the park. Other trails lead to the center of the park, and a longer, 4.6-mile trail winds around the west side of the lake.

REGULATIONS: No ground fires, plant removal, camping, frog hunting, tree cutting, firearms, bow hunting, animal collecting, or littering permitted.

HOURS: The park is open daily, 6:00 AM–10:00 PM. The environmental education center is open Monday–Friday, 8:30 AM–5:00 PM.

DIRECTIONS: From I-74, head south on IL 49 (exit 197) to 1350N, where there is a park sign. Head west on 1350N and follow the signs for 1.9 miles to the park entrance.

CONTACT INFORMATION: Salt Fork River Forest Preserve, 2573 S. Homer Lake Rd., Homer, IL 61849; (217) 896-2455; www.ccfpd.org/saltfork.htm

86. Kennekuk County Park

HIGHLIGHTS:

- *Middle Fork of the Vermilion River—Illinois's only Wild and Scenic River*
- *Visitor center with various exhibits and gift shop*
- *3,000-acre park*
- *180-acre lake*
- *2 Illinois Nature Preserves (84 acres)*
- *Lawrence Pioneer Cemetery*
- *Collins archaeological site, listed on the National Register of Historic Places*
- *Bunker Hill historic area*
- *Vermilion Conservationist newsletter*
- *Interpretive trails*

PROGRAMS AND EVENTS:

- *Overnight summer adventure program*
- *Haunted Happenings*
- *Outdoor Youth Adventure*
- *Outdoor school*
- *Adventure camp*
- *Summer night hikes*
- *Hunter safety course*

DESCRIPTION: Kennekuk County Park is just outside Danville in Vermilion County. The park features many large, mature oaks and hickories; a visitor center with various exhibits, live fish, stuffed animals, and archaeological artifacts; the Middle Fork of the Vermilion River—the only river in Illinois designated "wild and scenic"—flowing through it; a major archaeological site (the Collins site); various recreation facilities; a pioneer cemetery; a lake with a swimming beach; and a restored, historic village. Hiking trails scattered throughout the park total over 10 miles in length. A few of the shorter interpretive trails are discussed here.

The **Visitor Center Trail** is a .25-mile grass path that leads downhill to a restored prairie and connects with the **Cedar Hill Pond Trail,** which loops around the pond. Numerous birds and butterflies may be seen while hiking through this prairie.

The **Raccoon Run Trail** is a .5-mile loop marked with 15 numbered posts corresponding to descriptions in the interpretive brochure. The

Ironweed on shore of Cedar Hill Pond, Kennekuk County Park

trail starts near the earthen dam for Adrian Pond and then descends into a beautiful oak-hickory forest, looping back to the pond and the dam.

The **Look-Out Point Trail** is a loop through wooded and hilly terrain beginning at Oak Bluff Picnic Area. This .7-mile interpretive trail has 16 numbered posts and an associated interpretive brochure describing the flora and fauna in the area. The trail descends a steep set of stairs and then makes its way along a small creek, where there is a spectacular oak-hickory forest. It then heads up a hill and comes out to a clearing with a bench, a shelter, and an excellent view of the river floodplain. Be forewarned that the hilly terrain in this area can be strenuous and challenging in a few locations.

Other trails in the park include the **Hidden Valley Trail, River Bluff Trail,** and the 7-mile **Lake Mingo Trail** winding around the lake and past the Collins site.

REGULATIONS: Stay on trails.

HOURS: The visitor center is open Monday–Friday, 8:00 AM–4:30 PM; Saturday, 9:00 AM–4:00 PM; and Sunday, 12:00–4:00 PM. The park closes at 11:00 PM.

DIRECTIONS: From I-74, take the US 150–M. L. King Drive exit (exit 210). Follow US 150 east 1 mile to Henning Road, turn north, and go 4.7 miles to the park entrance on the west side of the road. The visitor center is 1 mile from the park entrance.

CONTACT INFORMATION: Kennekuk County Park, 22296-A Henning Rd., Danville, IL 61834; (217) 442-1691; www.vccd.org/recreation.html

87. Kickapoo State Park

HIGHLIGHTS:

- *Middle Fork of the Vermilion River—Illinois's only Wild and Scenic River*
- *2,800-acre reclaimed park*
- *69-acre Illinois Nature Preserve*
- *Hiking and accessible trails, horseback riding trails, and mountain biking trails*
- *Wildflowers*
- *100 bird species*
- *22 spring-fed strip mine ponds*

DESCRIPTION: Kickapoo State Park in Vermilion County is a 2,800-acre site that was formerly strip-mined for coal, and it is the first park in the nation built on reclaimed land. Today the park is a wooded tract with several clear ponds for fishing and scuba diving. The area once was home to the Kickapoo tribe, a village having been located near the confluence of the Middle Fork and Salt Fork rivers. Illinois's only Wild and Scenic River, the Middle Fork of the Vermilion flows through the center of the park and offers spectacular scenery as well as fishing and canoeing opportunities. The park has camping and picnicking facilities, a concession stand (seasonal), and a horseback riding rental facility, along with numerous hiking trails, a horse trail, and a mountain bike trail. A few of the shorter and accessible trails are described here.

The **High Lake Trail** (1.5 miles in length), southeast of the park office, is partly accessible, with a .25-mile, paved surface. The trail takes the visitor along the shore of High Lake, where there are great views of the lake as well as the wildflowers, and past the High Lake Day-Use Area, where a boat ramp, a shelter, rest rooms, and an accessible fishing pier are located. Past the day-use area, the trail turns to dirt as it goes up and down the old spoil banks and makes its way to the west end of the lake, where it connects with trails leading to the campground and with the Nature Trail.

The .75-mile **Nature Trail,** beginning at the Whitetail Day-Use Area, winds around the north side of High Lake. The trail passes through woods as it heads downhill towards the lake, where an overlook and bench are located; take precautions at the observation site, as the area is steep and eroded. Connecting trails lead to the campground and to the High Lake Trail.

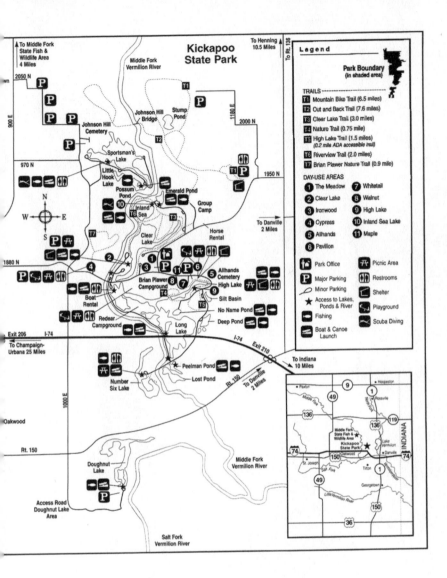

The **Brian Plawer Nature Trail,** named in honor of a former park superintendent, is at the west end of the park, west of the Vermilion River. The .75-mile trail takes the visitor to a remote part of the park and into the Middle Forks Woods Nature Preserve, an upland forest with numerous large oak trees. The trail heads down an old roadbed, and within .5 mile, a trail board may be seen. From here the trail loops through the nature preserve into a forest of oak, maple, and hickory along the edge of a small hill. Numerous wildflowers, birds, and other wildlife may be seen along this trail.

REGULATIONS: Stay on trails. Only electric motors may be used in lakes.

HOURS: The park is open daily, 8:00 AM–10:00 PM.

DIRECTIONS: From I-74, take exit 206. Head north on 850E to 1880N. Turn east and follow the road into the park.

CONTACT INFORMATION: Kickapoo State Park, 10906 Kickapoo Park Rd., Oakwood, IL 61858; (217) 442-4915; www.dnr.state.il.us/lands/landmgt/parks/r2/kickapoo.htm

88.   Forest Glen County Preserve

HIGHLIGHTS:
- *Nature center with various exhibits and caged animals outside*
- *Beech forest*
- *Doris L. Westfall Prairie Restoration Area*
- *1,800 acres of woodlands along the Vermilion River*
- *Arboretum*
- *Observation tower*
- *Ranger station*
- *Outdoor education center*
- *Pioneer homestead area*
- *4 Illinois Nature Preserves (Russell M. Duffin, Forest Glen Seep, Doris L. Westfall, and Howard's Hollow Seep) totaling 238 acres*
- *22 miles of trails, including an accessible trail, interpretive trails, and an 11.5-mile backpack trail*
- *Tree research area*

PROGRAMS AND EVENTS:
- *Traveling naturalist program*
- *Junior nature program*
- *Kids' fishing program*
- *Pioneer Kids*
- *Young Explorers Day Camp*
- *Leaf Collecting Hike*
- *Pioneer Craft Day*
- *Conservation Olympics*
- *Outdoor school (grades 4 and 5)*
- *Teacher workshops*
- *Bird walks, wildflower hikes, and hay rides*
- *Nature hikes*
- *Overnight summer adventure camp*
- *Senior citizen recreation camp*
- *Day, overnight, and sports camps*
- *Maple syrup open house*
- *Pancake and sausage dinner*
- *Revolutionary war reenactments*

DESCRIPTION: Forest Glen County Preserve, south of Danville in Vermilion County, is dominated by oak, hickory, and beech trees, some easily over 100 years old. The area borders the Vermilion River, and a

100-foot observation tower offers visitors an impressive view of the park and the river valley. A nature center, education center, 4 nature preserves, a restored prairie, a campground, and picnicking facilities provide numerous recreation opportunities and programs. A few of the shorter and more popular interpretive trails and an accessible trail are described here.

One of the most rugged trails in the park, the **Big Woods Trail** has to be one of the most scenic, too. The trail is .8 mile long and is marked as an interpretive trail. It follows the ravines in the area as it winds through the Duffin Nature Preserve, allowing great views of the beech and maple trees, Christmas ferns, and many spring and summer wildflowers. The trail goes up and down some small hills, over a small creek, and ultimately reaches the observation tower. The trail is marked with 15 numbered posts corresponding to a short write-up in the trail brochure. Two trail signs, one about woodland birds and the other on Native Americans, are found along the way. The Big Woods Trail also has a connection to the Beech Grove Trail.

The .3-mile, accessible (asphalt surface) **Beech Grove Trail** loops through an old growth oak and beech forest of towering trees, where there are benches and 15 numbered markers spaced along the trail corresponding to descriptions in a trail brochure.

The .25-mile **Doris Westfall Trail** is named after a conservationist who was instrumental in establishing the restored prairie and nature preserve in which the trail is located. The trail leads to an observation platform overlooking the prairie, where the numerous wildflowers and animals that are found in this area may be observed.

The 1.3-mile **Old Barn Trail,** beginning at the parking area for the park office (where there is also a trailhead for the **River Ridge Backpack Trail**) takes the visitor along the park lake for a short distance, where the lake views include a beaver dam at the lake's inlet. The trail has 15 numbered posts corresponding to descriptions in the park brochure, and 3 interpretive signs that tell about wetlands, bogs, and hawks may be seen along the trail. Some stairs and bridges are crossed, and then the trail goes through a successional forest and comes out at the tree research area.

The **Tall Tree Trail** (1 mile) and **Spring Crest Trail** (.3 mile) are next to each other in the parking area to the left of the observation tower. These trails are both loops through beech and oak forest and past some ravines. The Tall Tree Trail drops down to the floodplain where it joins with the River Ridge Backpack Trail for a short distance and then heads back uphill towards the parking area. Watch for wildflowers and wildlife along both trails.

The **Hawk Hill Trail** (less than 1 mile) leads to the observation tower and to the Vermilion River. The trail back from the river up to the observation tower is a steep climb. The Big Woods trailhead is on the right,

*Trail sign,
Forest Glen
County
Preserve*

just before the observation tower, which has a great view of the surrounding area.

REGULATIONS: No horses or bikes allowed on trails. Firearms, fireworks, and hunting are prohibited. All plants and animals are protected. Alcoholic beverages are allowed only at rental facilities or in designated picnic areas. Leash all pets.

HOURS: The park is open daily, 8:00 AM–10:00 PM. The park office is open Monday–Friday, 8:00 AM–4:30 PM. The nature center is open Sunday, 1:00–4:00 PM, between Memorial Day and Labor Day.

DIRECTIONS: From I-74, exit at US 150/IL 1 (Georgetown Road, exit 215A) in Danville. Follow US 150/IL 1 south 4.4 miles to Main Street in Westville. Turn east and follow the road for 7 miles to the park entrance on the left side of the road.

CONTACT INFORMATION: Forest Glen County Preserve, 20301 E 900 North Rd., Westville, IL 61883; (217) 662-2142; www.vccd.org/recreation.html

89.   Fall Creek Rest Area

HIGHLIGHTS:

- *Historic stone arch bridge, listed on the National Register of Historic Places*
- *Fall Creek and canyon*
- *Overlook of Mississippi River floodplain*
- *2 small waterfalls*
- *Partly accessible trail*

DESCRIPTION: Fall Creek Rest Area, owned and managed by the Illinois Department of Natural Resources, is 12 miles from Quincy in Adams County along the bluff line and floodplain of the Mississippi River. It has 2 sets of trails (totaling 2 miles in length), one heading along Fall Creek through the canyon to the historic bridge, and a second set that leads up to a bluff overlooking the floodplain of the river. On the Fall Creek portion, a paved trail leads from the lower parking facility up to the first waterfall, where there is an observation deck and a trail board. From here the visitor must walk the edge of the falls to get into the gorge, where there are some great views of the canyon walls. The trail then winds its way under the existing roadway and to the historic stone

Lower waterfall, Fall Creek Rest Area

arch bridge, built in 1855. Trails lead up onto the arch bridge and then an old roadbed and trail loops to the upper falls. The second set of trails consists of an old road and a narrow trail that lead up from the lower parking area to the bluff, where an observation platform overlooks the scenic floodplain. Use extreme caution while hiking in the canyon, on the historic bridge, and near the bluffs.

REGULATIONS: Stay on designated trails. Rock climbing and rappelling, ground fires, hunting, and camping are prohibited. Flowers, shrubs, trees, and other plants may not be removed or damaged. Leash all pets.

HOURS: The site is open daily, 7:00 AM–8:00 PM.

DIRECTIONS: From I-172, go southeast on IL 57 (exit 2) for .25 mile to Payson Road, where there is a sign for Fall Creek Rest Area. Turn left and go 3 blocks to the lower parking lot and picnic area.

CONTACT INFORMATION: Siloam Springs State Park, RR 1, Clayton, IL 62324; (217) 894-6205

90. Jenny Marr Memorial Park and Rexroat Prairie

HIGHLIGHTS:
  • *Restored prairie*
  • *1860 cabin*

DESCRIPTION: A small restored prairie and a pioneer cabin are to be found at the Jenny Marr Memorial Park, at the west end of Virginia in Cass County. The Rexroat Prairie was established in the mid-1970s and today has over 80 tallgrass prairie plant species. A .25-mile trail winds around the perimeter of the prairie and through the center of it on a mowed grass path, giving the visitor an idea of how the Prairie State used to look. Signs identify the plants found along the trail, which include purple prairie clover, compass plant, prairie dock, and cup plant. The cabin, originally from the Harry Dotzert farm and dating back to 1860, was donated and moved to its present site by Irene Rexroat in memory of Rollo Rexroat, a self-educated botanist who collected and identified many plant species. Prairie walks are held here in the summer.

Early evening in prairie, Jenny Marr Memorial Park and Rexroat Prairie

REGULATIONS: Walk on mowed grass paths only. No bikes allowed on the trail. No smoking permitted. No picking of flowers or grasses allowed.

HOURS: The site is open year-round.

DIRECTIONS: From IL 125 west of Springfield, turn south on IL 78 in Virginia, go 1 mile to Virginia Road, and turn right; a small parking lot is immediately to the right.

CONTACT INFORMATION: (217) 452-3729

91.   New Salem State Historic Site

HIGHLIGHTS:

- *Reconstructed New Salem pioneer village*
- *Visitor center with exhibits, auditorium, and outdoor amphitheater*
- *Interpretive trail with old cemetery, schoolhouse, and foundation ruins*
- *Archaeology walk with 6 interpretive displays*
- *Museum store*

PROGRAMS AND EVENTS:

- *School programs*
- *Discovery Series Workshops (e.g., Flora of New Salem, Birds of New Salem, Frontier Illinois, Making Shaker Boxes, Fiddler's Workshop, New Light on Lincoln's Years)*
- *Theater in the Park outdoor plays and musicals in the summer*
- *Apprentice interpreter*
- *Self-guided historic village tours*
- *Summer festival at New Salem (July)*
- *Prairie Tales at New Salem*
- *Traditional music festival*
- *Candlelight tour of New Salem (October)*
- *Historic demonstrations*
- *Surveying at New Salem*
- *Harvest feast at New Salem (November)*

DESCRIPTION: New Salem State Historic Site in Menard County is an 1830s village re-created from the times of Abraham Lincoln, who lived in New Salem for 6 years as a young man. The village consists of over 23 buildings, including a saw and grist mill on the Sangamon River. Visitors walk along the village road (accessible) to tour the buildings, many of which have volunteers dressed in costumes of the era. A visitor center provides some general information, exhibits on Lincoln and the reconstruction of New Salem, and an 18-minute audio presentation, as well as rest rooms, telephones, and water. A gift shop and fast-food restaurant are near the visitor center, while a formal sit-down restaurant may be found on the east side of IL 97. A museum shop is in the pioneer village. Two interpretive trails are described here.

The **Archaeology Walk** is the newest interpretive trail at the site. The wood-chip trail through the village is about 300 hundred feet in length,

Statue of Abraham Lincoln outside visitor center, New Salem State Historic Site

and the trailhead is behind the Second Barry Lincoln Store, where a display board can be found. In 1994, archaeologists uncovered additional buildings and an old roadbed that were overlooked in the initial survey of the village from the 1930s. Six interpretive signs along the trail describe the buildings that once stood on the grounds. And the old roadbed is now visible at the tree line, leading away from the village down the hillside.

The **Mentor Graham Trail** is a .75-mile interpretive trail that has 15 numbered posts corresponding to descriptions in a trail guide available at the visitor center. The trailhead is at the south end of the main parking area. The trail goes up and down the steep hills in the area, crossing the Rocky Branch Creek where a rock outcrop may be seen, and then makes a loop up a hill where there is an old school foundation, an old cemetery, and an old Scout building foundation. The trail then heads back down the hill and rejoins the main trail near the creek.

REGULATIONS: No flowers, shrubs, trees, or other plants may be removed or damaged. Do not feed animals. No littering. Children must be accompanied by adults.

HOURS: The village and visitor center are open daily, early April–late October, 9:00 AM–5:00 PM, and late October–early April, 8:00 AM–

4:00 PM; closed Tuesday and Wednesday in December, January, and February and on Thanksgiving, Christmas, and New Year's Day. The site closes at 10:00 PM.

DIRECTIONS: From I-55, take the Williamsville exit (exit 109) and head west for 7 miles to IL 29. Turn right (north) and go 1.7 miles to Athens, where signs for New Salem State Historic Site may be seen. Take a left and follow the road until it comes to a T. Turn right, go .2 mile, and turn left at the Athens Blacktop. Follow this road 7 miles to IL 97. Turn left and proceed .6 mile to the entrance on the right. From Springfield, follow IL 97 (Jefferson Street) west for 20 miles to the site entrance on the west side of the road. Turn left and head up the hill to the parking area. The visitor center is at the north end of the parking area.

CONTACT INFORMATION: New Salem State Historic Site, RR 1 Box 244A, Petersburg, IL 62675; (217) 632-4000; www.lincolnsnewsalem.com

92.   Meredosia National Wildlife Refuge

HIGHLIGHTS:
- *Accessible trail*
- *Wildlife observation deck with viewing scope*
- *Views of Meredosia Lake*
- *Numerous bird species*

DESCRIPTION: Meredosia Wildlife Refuge consists of 3,300 acres along the Illinois River and Meredosia Lake in Morgan County. The refuge is a haven for numerous bird species and a component of the Illinois River National Wildlife and Fish Refuges. A .25-mile nature trail leads the visitor through a prairie, a stand of pines, and to an observation deck overlooking Meredosia Lake. Wildlife-viewing binoculars and a bench are available here. Numerous waterfowl, wading birds, and shorebirds are known to feed and rest here. During the winter months, bald eagles are also seen in the vicinity. The trail surface is compacted gravel, making it fully accessible; but watch out for prickly pear cactus growing along the trail. A trail board at the trailhead describes the many bird species seen here.

Observation deck and viewing scope overlooking Meredosia Lake, Meredosia National Wildlife Refuge

REGULATIONS: Fires, overnight use, and camping are prohibited. Sport fishing and wildlife observation are permitted in areas open to public access. Nut, berry, and mushroom picking are allowed in areas open to the public.

HOURS: The refuge is open daily, sunrise to sunset.

DIRECTIONS: From IL 104 in Meredosia, turn north on North Putnam Street at the east end of town. Follow this road for 1 mile until a sign is seen on the left side of the road for the wildlife refuge. A gravel road leads to a small parking area.

CONTACT INFORMATION: Meredosia National Wildlife Refuge, Illinois River National Wildlife and Fish Refuges, 19031 E. County Rd., Havana, IL 62644; (309) 535-2290; midwest.fws.gov/illinoisriver/mer.html

93. Carpenter Park

HIGHLIGHTS:

- *350-acre upland and floodplain forest*
- *322-acre Illinois Nature Preserve*
- *Sandstone bedrock outcrops*
- *82 species of nesting birds*
- *Restored prairie*
- *Wildflowers*

DESCRIPTION: Carpenter Park is at the north end of Springfield in Sangamon County along the Sangamon River. The park has 350 acres of upland and floodplain forest along with over 30 acres of prairie, which have been restored with the assistance of the Sierra Club, the Nature Conservancy, and the Friends of the Sangamon Valley, a land trust. Ten connected trails (a total of 5 miles) wind through the upland and flood-

Hiking in autumn, Carpenter Park

plain ecosystems and past the prairie. White and black oaks are found in the upland forest, while sycamores, cottonwoods, and silver maples dominate the floodplain forest. Numerous wildflowers also may be seen here in the springtime. A large trail board at the parking area shows the trail layout. Some of the trails have wooden stairs that may be steep leading down to the river. Also, steep drops are encountered, and at times, portions of the trails may be inundated.

REGULATIONS: No camping allowed. All items protected by law.

HOURS: The park closes at dark.

DIRECTIONS: From I-55, exit at Sherman (exit 105). Head into Sherman and continue south on Peoria Road for 2.5 miles and turn right at the south end of the golf course on the west side of the road. Follow this road straight into the park.

CONTACT INFORMATION: Springfield Park District, 2500 S. Eleventh St., PO Box 5052, Springfield, IL 62705; (217) 544-1751

94.   Adams Wildlife Sanctuary

HIGHLIGHTS:
- *Nature center with exhibits*
- *Prairie restoration site*
- *Bird observation room*
- *Interpretive trail with 20 numbered posts
  and map guide*

PROGRAMS AND EVENTS:
- *Nature Explorers Program*
- *Discovery Hikes*
- *Project Wild Activities*
- *School field trips*
- *Scout and youth group activities*

DESCRIPTION: Adams Wildlife Sanctuary is a 30-acre site in an urban setting on the east side of Springfield in Sangamon County. Formerly a prairie and then farmed, the site has been relatively untouched for the past 50 years. Given to the Illinois Audubon Society in 1983 upon the death of the former property owner, Margery Adams, it has been converted into a nature center, a trail system has been built, and a prairie has been transformed on the property. There are 2 main loop trails, with 20 trail markers corresponding to descriptions on a trail map. **Margery's Trail** may be started outside the nature center and loops for .25 mile. It joins the **Woodland Trail** (1 mile), which may be taken north towards the 3-acre prairie. Large cottonwoods and silver maples may be seen through the woodlands, and wildflowers such as goldenrod, rattlesnake master, black-eyed susan, and blazing star may appear in the prairie. There are benches along the trail under the tree canopy. The trail loops back to the nature center or connects with a short trail spur to the parking area. The sanctuary may be visited year-round; spring through fall is a good time to visit as various wildflowers are in bloom. Call ahead for information on the hours of operation and programs offered at the nature center.

REGULATIONS: No food, drinks, alcohol, smoking, pets, horses, fires, firearms, motorized vehicles, or bicycles permitted. Stay on the trail. No hunting, trapping, or collecting allowed.

HOURS: The trails are open daily, sunrise to sunset.

DIRECTIONS: From I-55 in Springfield, take Clear Lake Avenue (exit 98B) west for 1.6 miles until a sign is seen for the entrance to the sanctuary on the north side of the road. Turn right into the parking lot.

CONTACT INFORMATION: 2315 E. Clear Lake Ave., Springfield, IL 62703; (217) 544-5781; www.springfield.k12.il.us/adamswildlife

95.   Lincoln Memorial Garden and Nature Center

HIGHLIGHTS:
- *Nature center with displays, animal exhibits, live fish, and shop carrying books, gifts, and crafts*
- *Building designed by landscape architect Jens Jensen, listed on the National Register of Historic Places*
- *Cypress grove*
- *Ostermeier Prairie Center*
- *Restored prairies*
- *Wildflowers*
- *Nature, interpretive, and accessible trails*
- *Wildlife viewing*
- Nature Center News *newsletter*
- *225-year-old chinkapin oak tree*

PROGRAMS AND EVENTS:
- *Naturalist and junior naturalist programs*
- *Maple Syrup Time*
- *Indian Summer Festival (October)*
- *Summer Ecology Camp*
- *Holiday Market*
- *Wildflower hikes*
- *Prairie plant and wildflower sale*
- *Prairie seed collecting workshop*
- *Leaf and tree identification hike*
- *Sausage and pancake breakfast*
- *Breakfast hike*
- *Moonlight hike*

DESCRIPTION: Lincoln Memorial Garden and Nature Center, along the shores of Lake Springfield in Sangamon County, was designed by the famous landscape architect Jens Jensen as a living memorial to President Lincoln. The grounds consist of 107 acres of rolling hills, oaks, maples, prairies, wildflowers, a nature center and bookstore, and beautiful trails winding through the grounds. The newest portion of the site is the 30-acre Ostermeier Property, which has a pond, a restored prairie, connecting trails to the main garden property, and a 1-mile accessible trail (packed gravel) that goes around the pond and a prairie. The pond has a wildlife viewing area and an overlook. A shorter, self-guided interpretive trail with 18 numbered stations (and an associated brochure)

165

Lincoln Memorial Garden Trail Map

NORTH

LAKE SPRINGFIELD

WALNUT TRAIL

BIRD CHERRY TRAIL

BIRD CHERRY TRAIL

BEECH TRAIL

WILD FLOWER TRAIL

CYPRESS GROVE

FRINGE TREE TRAIL

ARROW WOOD TRAIL

To I-55 / St. Rt. 29 (1 mile)

PRAIRIE PATH

PARKING LOT

SHEEP BERRY LANE

RED BUD LANE

LAKE TRAIL

WHITE OAK TRAIL

LINCOLN COUNCIL RING

CRAB APPLE LANE

SILVER BELL TRAIL

MAIN PARKING LOT

EAST LAKE DRIVE

PRAIRIE ROAD

SEASONAL PARKING

WALNUT AND OAK GROVE

RED BUD TRAIL

DOGWOOD LANE

BIRCH LANE

NATURE CENTER

LAKE TRAIL

BUCKEYE TRAIL

MAPLE LANE

SASSAFRAS LANE

WALGREEN BRIDGE

HICKORY LANE

PARKING LOT

To I-55 / St. Rt. (1 mile)

SHADY LANE

HAWTHORNE TRAIL

WITCH HAZEL TRAIL

MEADOW

HIGH

OSTERMEIER PRAIRIE CENTER

BARN & GREENHOUSE

POND

FARM HOUSE

LEGEND

- ◯ COUNCIL RING
- ▦ BRIDGE
- ◆ DRINKING FOUNTAIN
- ▦ PRAIRIE RESTORATION AREA
- ∿ STREAM
- — PROPERTY BOUNDARY
- — WALKING PATH
- ⬥ ACCESSIBLE PATH
- ⁖ WILDLIFE OBSERVATION AREA
- ❄ PRAIRIE OBSERVATION AREA
- ★ RESTROOMS
- ⊼ PICNIC SHELTER
- ⫟ TREE LINE / FENCE ROW

Please Note:

Picking or collecting of any kind is strictly prohibited without permission of Garden staff. All visitors must stay on the marked trails. No alcohol, bicycles, fishing or fires permitted.

APPROXIMATE DISTANCE FROM NATURE CENTER TO:

LINCOLN COUNCIL RING – 1/4 MILE
WALGREEN BRIDGE – 1/4 MILE
CYPRESS GROVE – 2/8+ MILE
OSTERMEIER PRAIRIE CENTER – 3/4 MILE

loops around the property, starting and ending at the nature center. One of the highlights of the gardens is the 225-year-old chinkapin oak tree.

REGULATIONS: No picking of anything, including collecting of flowers, nuts, mushrooms, driftwood, and so on. Stay on trails. No dogs, alcohol, bicycles, fishing, or fires permitted.

HOURS: The grounds are open daily, sunrise to sunset. The visitor center is open Tuesday–Saturday, 10:00 AM–4:00 PM; Sunday, 1:00–4:00 PM; closed on Monday.

DIRECTIONS: From I-55 southbound, take the East Lake Drive/ Stevenson Drive exit (exit 94) in Springfield and travel east on East Lake Drive for 6 miles to the entrance on the right side of the road. From I-55 northbound, take the Chatham/East Lake Drive exit (exit 88) and go east on East Lake Drive for 3 miles; the entrance will be on the left.

CONTACT INFORMATION: Lincoln Memorial Garden and Nature Center, 2301 E. Lake Dr., Springfield, IL 62707; (217) 529-1111; www.lmgnc.com

96. Rock Springs Center for Environmental Discovery

HIGHLIGHTS:
- *1,343 acres of prairies and woodland*
- *Visitor center with various exhibits, Children's Awareness Room, gift shop, museum, bird window, and information*
- *Homestead Prairie Farm, listed on the National Register of Historic Places*
- *Restored prairie*
- *Bird-feeding station*
- *8 miles of trails with an interpretive, accessible prairie path and bike path*
- Prairie Islander *newsletter*
- *Lookout tower*

PROGRAMS AND EVENTS:
- *Earth adventure program*
- *Prairie celebration*
- *1860s Fourth of July*
- *Various demonstrations and workshops*
- *Maple syrup program*

DESCRIPTION: The Rock Springs Center for Environmental Discovery is a wooded tract bordered by the Sangamon River near Decatur in Macon County. The park consists of 1,343 acres of upland and floodplain woodlands and restored prairies. The visitor center has numerous exhibits on plants and animals, rocks and minerals, and Native Americans in addition to the many programs and classes held there. At the Homestead Prairie Farm, an 1860s farmhouse is featured. On the grounds are more than 8 miles of trails, including an accessible, paved, 2-mile bike path leading to Fairview Park.

The **Discovery Trail** is a short interpretive trail west of the visitor center. This trail has 11 numbered posts corresponding to descriptions in the trail brochure (spring or fall versions). The trail loops through a woodland, past a pond, over the bike trail, past a restored prairie, and through a forest of red and white pines. A good way to see a prairie is to take the **Prairie Path** east of the visitor center. This trail heads east towards the Homestead Prairie Farm, where visitors can explore a restored farmstead. A self-guiding brochure identifies the many wildflowers found along the way. The 2.25-mile **River Trail** is recommended for cross-country skiing.

REGULATIONS: No alcohol or firearms allowed. No horses or vehicles permitted on trails. Leash pets. Bicycles restricted to surface trails only. No collecting of plants or animals allowed. Picnics and fires permitted in designated areas only.

HOURS: The trails are open daily, 8:00 AM to dusk. The visitor center is open Monday–Saturday, 9:00 AM–4:30 PM; and Sunday, 1:00–4:30 PM.

DIRECTIONS: From I-72 in Decatur, go east on US 36 (exit 30A) to Wyckles Road. Turn south, go 3 miles, and turn left on County Road 10. Go about 1 mile, take a left, and follow the signs to the visitor center.

CONTACT INFORMATION: Rock Springs Center for Environmental Discovery, 1495 Brozio Ln., Decatur, IL 62521; (217) 423-7708; www.fgi.net/~mccd/rock.htm

97.   Spitler Woods State Natural Area

HIGHLIGHTS:
- *Old growth oak-maple-hickory forest*
- *146-acre Illinois Nature Preserve*
- *Accessible and interpretive trail*
- *Numerous bird species*
- *Wildflowers*

DESCRIPTION: Spitler Woods State Natural Area is a 202-acre forested tract near Decatur in Macon County named in honor of Ida B. Spitler, who donated the property to the state to be preserved. The Spitler Woods Nature Preserve comprises almost three-quarters of the park and is the home of 2 hiking trails, which begin south of the park office. The .5-mile, accessible **Red Oak Ramble Trail,** which has a gravel surface, makes a short loop around relatively flat terrain and past some fine oak trees. It joins the longer, 2-mile **Squirrel Creek Trail,** a dirt path that winds around the nature preserve, going up and down the hilly terrain, over some bridges and Squirrel Creek, and into a floodplain. A forest of oak, maple, and hickory is passed through and numerous bird species may be seen as the trail heads towards the first picnic shelter in the park. A .5-mile physical fitness trail is also found at the park.

REGULATIONS: Stay on trails. Leash dogs. Bikes prohibited on trails. No camping, ground fires, picking of flowers or leaves, harvesting of nuts or mushrooms, or gathering of firewood permitted.

HOURS: The site is open daily, 8:00 AM–10:00 PM.

DIRECTIONS: From US 36 east out of Decatur, turn south on IL 121 and travel 2.6 miles to Spitler Park Drive. Head east for .5 mile to the park entrance on the right.

CONTACT INFORMATION: Spitler Woods State Natural Area, 705 Spitler Park Dr., Mount Zion, IL 62549; (217) 864-3121; www.dnr.state.il.us/lands/landmgt/parks/r3/spitler.htm

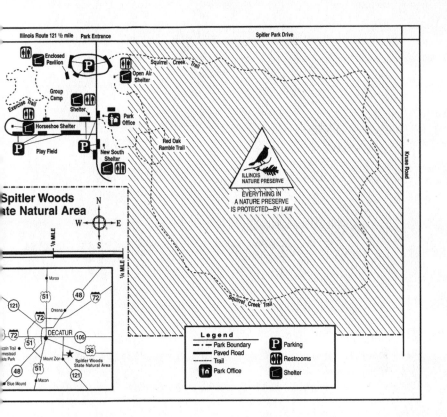

Illinois Route 121 ½ mile   Park Entrance   Spitler Park Drive

Enclosed Pavilion

Open Air Shelter

Group Camp

Shelter

Exercise Trail

Horseshoe Shelter

Park Office

Red Oak Ramble Trail

Play Field

New South Shelter

Squirrel Creek Trail

ILLINOIS NATURE PRESERVE

EVERYTHING IN
A NATURE PRESERVE
IS PROTECTED—BY LAW

Kruse Road

**Spitler Woods
State Natural Area**

N
W   E
S

⅛ MILE

¼ MILE

Maroa

51   48   72

121

72

Oreana

72

DECATUR   105

51

Lincoln Trail
Homestead
State Park

72

36

Mount Zion

Spitler Woods
State Natural Area

48   51

121

Macon

Blue Mound

Squirrel Creek Trail

Legend

— · — Park Boundary	**P** Parking
—— Paved Road	Restrooms
-------- Trail	
Park Office	Shelter

98.   Walnut Point State Park

HIGHLIGHTS:
- *Interpretive trail*
- *Nature trail in the 65-acre Upper Embarras Woods Nature Preserve*
- *59-acre lake*
- *Old growth forest*
- *Spring wildflowers (more than 200 species)*
- *Restored prairie*

DESCRIPTION: Walnut Point State Park, a 592-acre site in southeastern Douglas County, features the 59-acre Walnut Point Lake, campgrounds, various picnic facilities, some of the oldest old growth forest left in the area, and 2 trails. The **Lakeside Nature Trail** is a .5-mile interpretive trail with a small restored prairie near the parking area, some great lake views, a few benches, and 9 numbered fiberglass posts identifying the trees in a mature forest of sycamore, white oak, black oak, northern red oak, and shagbark hickory, many of which are between 100 and 150 years old. There are also several good access points to the lake for fishing. A trail booklet is available from the park staff. **Whispering Pines Nature Trail** is a 1.75-mile trail that begins near the entrance to the campground; the trailhead and a trail board may be found directly across the street from the Pleasant View Picnic Area. The trail then turns away from the park road and into the Upper Embarras Nature Preserve, where there are an old growth forest and, in the spring, numerous wildflowers. The trail loops through the nature preserve towards the Embarras River, where a short connecting spur leads down to the river; use caution during flood events. The trail then crosses a large stairway and goes back up the hillside. Numerous white and black oaks are encountered along this trail, as well as pines, ferns, and various wildflowers such as trillium and bloodroot.

REGULATIONS: No swimming allowed. Leash all pets. Foot traffic permitted on trails only. Only electric motors may be used on lake. Park in designated areas only. Fires allowed only in grills. No cutting of trees allowed.

HOURS: The park is open daily, 7:00 AM–10:00 PM.

DIRECTIONS: From I-57, take IL 133 (exit 203) east for 14 miles to Oakland. Turn north on North Walnut Street and travel 3 miles to

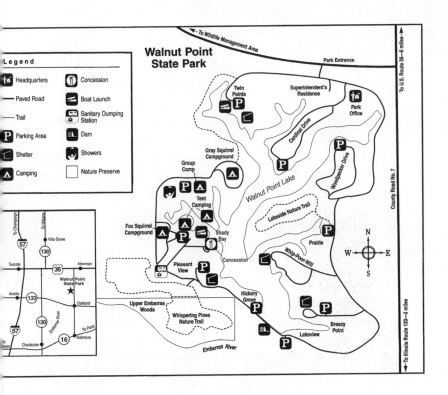

375N. Turn west and proceed a few blocks to the park entrance. Lakeside Nature Trail may be found .7 mile past the park office, while Whispering Pines Nature Trail is 1 mile further on.

CONTACT INFORMATION: Walnut Point State Park, RR 2 Box 250, Oakland, IL 61943; (217) 346-3336; www.dnr.state.il.us/lands/landmgt/parks/r3/walnutpt.htm

99.   Anderson Prairie Park

HIGHLIGHTS:

- *Restored prairie*
- *Observation tower*
- *Wildflower trail with 42 numbered stations*
- *Numerous birds and butterflies*
- *Outdoor laboratory and butterfly display*
- *Rail-to-trail conversion*

DESCRIPTION: Anderson Prairie Park, in Pana (Christian County), is a 25-acre park and restored prairie currently managed by Dave Nance, a biology teacher at Pana High School. Named after Vernon Anderson, who taught biology in Pana, and owned by the City of Pana and the Pana School District, it serves as an outdoor laboratory for students and visitors. At the site is a 1-mile trail that follows some abandoned railroad tracks into the restored prairie and a wildflower area that attracts about 50 species of birds and 60 species of butterflies, as well as bees. Over 300 plant species have been recorded in the prairie, and according to Nance, the "prairie is being managed as it existed in presettlement times." There is also the short **Butterfly Trail** with a trail board and trail map at

Observation tower and information board, Anderson Prairie Park

the start and 42 numbered stations in the prairie. Near this trail is an observation platform to view the prairie. Spring through late fall is a good time to explore the converted rail-to-trail path that goes past the prairie, through some wooded areas, and to the outskirts of town.

REGULATIONS: No disturbing or harming any plants or animals allowed. Motorized vehicles, firearms, explosive devices, and alcoholic beverages are prohibited.

HOURS: The park is open daily, dawn to dusk.

DIRECTIONS: Take US 51 or IL 16 west to Pana. Turn south on Locust Street and go 1 mile to 9th Street, head west to Chestnut, turn south, and proceed .6 mile to the parking area found on the left side of the road.

CONTACT INFORMATION: Pana High School, 201 W. 8th, Pana, IL 62557; (217) 562-3589 or (217) 245-1886

100.   Eagle Creek State Park

HIGHLIGHTS:
- *Oak-hickory forest*
- *Wildflowers*
- *Birds and other wildlife*
- *Lake Shelbyville*
- *Eagle Creek Resort and Conference Center*

DESCRIPTION: Eagle Creek State Park and the Eagle Creek Resort and Conference Center are in Shelby County. The **Ridge Nature Trail** offers the visitor a chance to explore the oak-hickory forest, some small ravines, and the shores of Lake Shelbyville. There are some beautiful old trees, numerous mammals including deer, many birds, and wildflowers in the spring and summer months. The loop trail has 30 numbered posts corresponding to short descriptions in a brochure available at the lodge. There are benches along the trail, some wooden bridges to cross, and opportunities for fishing in the lake. The state park also has a golf course, camping, picnicking, hiking, boat ramps, a lodge and restaurant, and an 11-mile backpack trail (**Chief Illini Trail**).

REGULATIONS: Stay on trail. Leash all pets.

HOURS: The park is open year-round.

DIRECTIONS: From IL 121 east of Decatur, turn south on IL 128 and travel 8 miles to Bruce Findlay Road. Turn east and travel to 2100N. Turn south and travel 2 miles to the park entrance. Ridge Nature Trail is next to the resort. Visitors can park in the main parking area.

CONTACT INFORMATION: Eagle Creek State Park, RR 1 PO Box 6, Findlay, IL 62534; (217) 756-8260; www.dnr.state.il.us/lands/landmgt/parks/r3/eaglecrk.htm

101. Hidden Springs State Forest

HIGHLIGHTS:
- *1,200 acres in 3 separate wooded tracts*
- *7 springs*
- *Interpretive trails*
- *Wildflowers*

DESCRIPTION: Hidden Springs State Forest is composed of 3 separate tracts of land totaling 1,200 acres located 10 miles southeast of Shelbyville in Shelby County. Named for the several springs within its bounds, it is comprised of upland and bottomland forest and floodplain along Richland Creek. Beautiful oaks and hickories, as well as numerous wildflowers, abound in the park. Among the many recreation facilities are 3 main hiking trails.

The **Big Tree Nature Trail** is at the eastern end of the forest. This 1-mile interpretive trail contains 30 numbered posts corresponding to descriptions found in a trail brochure. The trail loops through a tract with wildflowers and old trees, including a large sycamore with a 76-inch diameter and 116 feet tall. The trail goes up and down some small hills and draws to an overlook of the creek, where there is a small wooden fence along the edge. Directly across the parking area for the trail is Quicksand Spring, 1 of the 2 accessible springs.

The **Possum Hollow Interpretive Nature Trail** is 3 miles southwest of the Big Tree Nature Trail off County Road 700N. The trail begins behind the forest headquarters down the hill, where there is a trail board. This .75-mile interpretive trail has 35 numbered posts corresponding to descriptions in the trail brochure. The trail winds around a small creek and wooded area, and connecting trails lead to a campground, a picnic area, and a pond. Numerous tree species and some benches may be found along this trail.

The **Rocky Spring Nature Trail** is 2.5 miles southwest of the forest office and just south of County Road 600N. This trail is a 3-mile loop on dirt and an old roadbed that winds its way through a beautiful oak and hickory upland forest to Richland Creek, where it follows the edge of the bluff line, and to Rocky Spring.

REGULATIONS: Leash pets. Swimming prohibited. Keep vehicles on roads, pads, or parking lots. Keep motorcycles and horses off the foot trails and fire lanes. Removal of flowers, shrubs, trees, or other plants is prohibited. Put litter in trash cans.

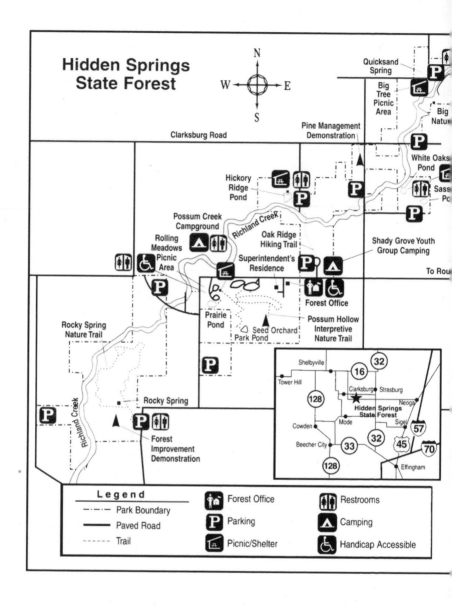

Hidden Springs State Forest

Quicksand Spring

Big Tree Picnic Area

Big Natu...

Clarksburg Road

Pine Management Demonstration

White Oaks Pond

Hickory Ridge Pond

Sass... Po...

Possum Creek Campground

Richland Creek

Oak Ridge Hiking Trail

Rolling Meadows Picnic Area

Superintendent's Residence

Shady Grove Youth Group Camping

To Rou...

Prairie Pond

Seed Orchard
Park Pond

Possum Hollow Interpretive Nature Trail

Forest Office

Rocky Spring Nature Trail

Richland Creek

Rocky Spring

Forest Improvement Demonstration

Shelbyville

Tower Hill

16

32

128

Clarksburg   Strasburg

Neoga

Hidden Springs State Forest

Cowden

Mode

Sige...

57

Beecher City

33

32

45

70

128

Effingham

Legend

–··–··– Park Boundary
——— Paved Road
- - - - - Trail

👥 Forest Office

🅿 Parking

⛺ Picnic/Shelter

🚻 Restrooms

⛺ Camping

♿ Handicap Accessible

HOURS: The site is open daily, 6:00 AM–10:00 PM.

DIRECTIONS: From IL 16 east of Shelbyville, turn south at 2550E and travel 4.5 miles to the Big Tree Trail parking area in the easternmost tract of the forest.

CONTACT INFORMATION: Hidden Springs State Forest, Box 200 RFD 1, Strasburg, IL 62465; (217) 644-3091; www.dnr.state.il.us/lands/landmgt/parks/hiddensp/r3/hsforest.htm

102.   Douglas-Hart Nature Center

HIGHLIGHTS:
- *Visitor center with various animals, bird observation area, hands-on exhibits, and gift shop*
- *67 acres of natural habitat*
- *Interpretive trail*
- *Pond observation area*
- The Nuthatch News *newsletter*
- *Restored prairie*
- *Picnic area bird garden*
- *Butterfly garden*

PROGRAMS AND EVENTS:
- *Bird Roosting Box Workshop*
- *Owl Prowl*
- *Wild Birds and Prey*
- *Project Wild*
- *Winter Celebration and Open House*
- *Nature study classes (e.g., Budding Naturalists, Little Explorers, Nature Nuts, Eco-Adventures, Wild Adventure Days)*
- *Weekly bird walks*
- *Nature field trips*
- *Summer campfires*
- *Teacher workshops*
- *Naturalist in the classroom*

DESCRIPTION: The Douglas-Hart Nature Center, on the east side of Mattoon in Coles County, is a nature education facility with an associated interpretive trail system where numerous programs are offered for the public throughout the year. The grounds are named after Helen Douglas-Hart, who helped to develop a natural area here that would be set aside for native habitats typical of central Illinois. Today, the grounds consist of 67 acres of native tree plantings (over 50 species), a restored prairie, and a small wetland complex. A 2-mile, interpretive, wood-chip and dirt trail winds through these habitats past 21 numbered stations corresponding to descriptions in a self-guided trail booklet. Numerous tree species are identified along the trail, which leads to a small pond and wetland area with a bird observatory and overlook. Over 150 bird species are found in this area, including owls, hawks, nuthatches, and woodpeckers.

Hands-on exhibits, Douglas-Hart Nature Center

REGULATIONS: Do not remove or damage any plants or animals. Motorized vehicles and bicycles prohibited on trails. Picnicking allowed only on tables by the visitor center. Leash all pets. No fishing allowed.

HOURS: The trails are open daily, dawn to dusk. The visitor center is open Monday–Saturday, 8:00 AM–4:00 PM; and Sunday, 1:00–4:00 PM.

DIRECTIONS: From I-57 at Mattoon, head east on IL 16 (exit 190) for 1 mile to Lerna Road. Turn north and go .6 mile to County Road 316 (800N). Turn west and proceed 2 blocks to the entrance on the north side of the road.

CONTACT INFORMATION: Douglas-Hart Nature Center, 2204 DeWitt Ave. E., Mattoon, IL 61938; (217) 235-4644; www.advant.com/users/dhnature

103.   Fox Ridge State Park

HIGHLIGHTS:
- *Wooded tract*
- *Accessible trail*

DESCRIPTION: Fox Ridge State Park is south of Charleston and the campus of Eastern Illinois University in Coles County. This wooded tract along the Embarras River offers many recreation facilities, including 8 miles of hiking trails. The .25-mile, paved, accessible **Oakridge Trail** is a shared-fitness trail that parallels the edge of a wooded ravine and goes between the White Pines and Possum Holler picnic areas.

REGULATIONS: No swimming or ground fires allowed. All-terrain vehicles and bicycles prohibited on trails.

HOURS: The park is open daily, 7:30 AM–5:00 PM.

DIRECTIONS: From I-57 at Mattoon, go east on IL 16 (exit 190) through Charleston. Turn south on IL 130 and go 6.5 miles to the park entrance.

CONTACT INFORMATION: Fox Ridge State Park, 18175 State Park Rd., Charleston, IL 61920; (217) 345-6416; www.dnr.state.il.us/lands/landmgt/parks/fox/fox.htm

104. McCully Heritage Project

HIGHLIGHTS:
- *Interpretive trail*
- *Mid-1800s log cabin*
- *Observation platform overlooking the Illinois River valley*
- *940-acre site*
- *Fishing pond*

DESCRIPTION: The McCully Heritage Project consists of 940 acres of woods and hills overlooking the lower Illinois River valley just south of Kampsville in Calhoun County. The property was donated by Howard and Eva McCully and is now operated by the nonprofit McCully Heritage Project Foundation. The site is open to the public for the purposes of enjoying nature and exploration. Twelve miles of trails wind their way through the grounds. The 1.5-mile interpretive trail is comprised of 2 connecting loops, the **Grassland Loop** and the **Woodland Loop.** At the parking area, visitors should register at the kiosk and pick up the available trail guide. The interpretive trail system starts near the rest

Mid-1800s log cabin, McCully Heritage Project

182

rooms, heads north, and soon comes to a log cabin, which is over 150 years old, and a gravestone for the McCullys. The trail continues on to a small fishing pond with a gazebo and a shelter nearby. The Woodland Loop goes around the pond, while the Grassland Loop continues north up a hill to a viewing platform overlooking the river valley, passes through some wooded areas, and finally joins the Woodland Loop and heads south towards the parking lot. Primitive camping is available by permission.

REGULATIONS: No horseback riding allowed October 1–December 31. Stay on designated trail. All children to be accompanied by an adult. No swimming permitted in the ponds. No pets or wheeled vehicles allowed on the trails. No smoking. No collecting or disturbing any features allowed.

HOURS: The site is open daily, 8:00 AM to dark.

DIRECTIONS: From IL 100 in Kampsville, go 1 mile south to 2930N (Crawford Creek Road), where there is a sign for McCully Heritage Project. Proceed west on 2930N for 1 mile. Parking is on the north side of the road.

CONTACT INFORMATION: McCully Heritage Project, Route 1, Kampsville, IL 62053; (618) 653-4687

105. Shoal Creek Nature Conservation Area

HIGHLIGHTS:
- *Wildflowers*
- *Restored prairie*
- *Barrens-savanna habitat*
- *276 natural acres along Lake Lou Yeager*
- *Interpretive trail*
- *613 plant species and 64 butterfly species*

DESCRIPTION: Shoal Creek Nature Conservation Area is a wooded tract owned by the City of Litchfield along Lake Lou Yeager in Montgomery County. The area consists of 276 acres, which include a restored prairie, a barrens-savanna habitat (rocky area with little woody vegetation and grassland with some trees), and succession woodlands. Two loop trails (A and B) forming the .8-mile, dirt surfaced **Rotary Trail** wind through the various habitats, up and down rolling hills, by the lake, and past a restored prairie. Numbered posts along each trail segment correspond to descriptions in the trail brochure, which is available at the trailhead. White blazes on trees identify the various tree species, and there are numerous bluebird houses that were installed through the efforts of the Litchfield Rotary Club.

REGULATIONS: No motorized vehicles, bicycles, or horses permitted.

HOURS: The site is open only during daylight for safety.

DIRECTIONS: From I-55, head east on IL 16 in Litchfield (exit 52) for 2.8 miles to Yeager Lake Trail Road. Turn north and follow the road for 2.5 miles, passing by Lake Lou Yeager, where a trail board will be seen on the left side of the road. Parking is next to the road.

CONTACT INFORMATION: City of Litchfield, 120 E. Ryder St., Litchfield, IL 62056; (217) 324-2022

106. Pere Marquette State Park

HIGHLIGHTS:
- *Second largest state park in Illinois*
- *Lodge and cabins*
- *Visitor center with exhibits, information, programs, gift shop, and meeting room*
- *8,000-acre park with bluff-top views of the Illinois River floodplain*
- *15 miles of trails*
- *Scenic overlooks*
- *Rock formations*
- *Indian mounds*
- *Wildflowers*
- *Restored prairie*

PROGRAMS AND EVENTS:
- *Wetland programs*
- *Owl Program*
- *Wild Edible Food Program*
- *Scavenger Hunts*
- *Eagle tours*
- *Nature hikes*

DESCRIPTION: Pere Marquette State Park in Jersey County, the second largest state park in Illinois with nearly 8,000 acres, is near Grafton, close to the confluence of the Illinois and Mississippi rivers. The park consists of rolling terrain and bluffs above the river with spectacular scenery. The park lodge was built by the Civilian Conservation Corps in the 1930s, and there are cabins for overnight lodging. A new visitor center has numerous exhibits, information, and gifts. Nearly 15 miles of hiking trails wind through the park.

To get a good feel for the park, visitors can take **A Walk in the Woods Self-Guided Hike,** which begins outside the visitor center and leads up the **Ravine Trail** to the top of the bluffs towards McAdams Peak, Twin Mounds, and the Twin Shelters. There is a restored prairie on top of the bluff near these landmarks. McAdams Peak has an observation deck / shelter overlooking the river valley. In the early 1930s, this area was excavated and Native American remains were removed to the Smithsonian Institute. The Twin Mounds are burial sites that have been preserved near a restored prairie. Visitors can follow the **Hickory Trail** west along the ridge top to the **Ridge Trail,** which leads back to the visitor center.

REGULATIONS: Leash all pets. All items protected by law.

HOURS: The park is open only during daylight for safety.

DIRECTIONS: From Grafton, go 5 miles west on IL 100 to the park.

CONTACT INFORMATION: Pere Marquette State Park, Route 100, PO Box 158, Grafton, IL 62037; (618) 786-3323; www.dnr.state.il.us/lands/landmgt/parks/r4/peremarq.htm

107.   Gordon F. Moore Community Park

HIGHLIGHTS:
- *Accessible and interpretive trails*
- *Oriental garden with small waterfall*
- *Lake*
- *Waterwheel*
- *Golf course and other recreation facilities*
- *Rose garden*
- *Restored prairie with over 130 plant species*
- *Wildflowers*
- *Numerous butterflies and birds*

DESCRIPTION: The Gordon F. Moore Community Park, in Alton (Madison County), is home to a number of recreation facilities. Along a .25-mile, paved, accessible trail, there are benches and braille signs that identify the trees and the tree habitats in the area. A set of guide ropes leads the visitor to each braille sign station, and a knot in the rope indicates when the sign is near. Along this trail is a beautiful oriental garden with a small waterfall, a pond, and a pagoda. A wooden bridge that spans an arm of the lake leads to a waterwheel.

Directly across IL 140 is a 27-acre restored prairie and trail system known as the **Nature Institute Prairie Trail.** Over 130 plant species are found here, including bluestem, compass plant, rattlesnake master, blazing star, and wild white indigo, along with many bird and butterfly species. The trail system consists of a series of loops in the prairie/wildflower area along mowed grass paths. The total trail length is about 1.25 miles, and there is a .25-mile interpretive loop that features 14 numbered posts corresponding to descriptions of the flora and fauna in the guide booklet available from the Nature Institute.

REGULATIONS: Speed limit is 20 miles per hour through the park. No alcohol, swimming, skateboards, or skates allowed. Stay on designated trails.

HOURS: The park is open daily, daylight to dusk.

DIRECTIONS: From I-55, take IL 140 west (exit 30) for 15.5 miles to Alton. Three miles west of the IL 111/140 junction is the entrance to the park, on the south side of IL 140. Follow the road into the park, turn right at the T, and go .6 mile to the parking area near the lake. To reach

Accessible braille nature trail, Gordon F. Moore Community Park

the Nature Institute Prairie Trail on the north side of IL 140, turn north on McDuffy Street and go .2 mile to the trail board, where there is a sign for the trail.

CONTACT INFORMATION: Alton Parks and Recreation Department, 1211 Henry St., Alton, IL 62002; (618) 463-3580

The Nature Institute, 2213 South Levis Ln., Godfrey, IL 62035; (618) 466-9930

108.   Watershed Nature Center

HIGHLIGHTS:
- *Nature center with various exhibits and animals*
- *Partly accessible trail*
- *Wetlands with observation decks and boardwalk*
- *Restored prairie*
- Watershed News *newsletter*

PROGRAMS AND EVENTS:
- *Seasonal programs (e.g., Aquatic Bug Day, Frog Walk,
  Bird Watching, Wildflower Walks)*

DESCRIPTION: The Watershed Nature Center in Madison County is owned by the City of Edwardsville and operated by the Nature Preserve Foundation. It has various exhibits and programs and features wetlands and a prairie. A 1.5-mile set of trails goes around the wetland complex, and another set of trails follows an old abandoned railroad track above the grounds. An accessible portion of the trail to the left of the nature center leads to the wetlands, and a concrete boardwalk over part of the wetlands offers a good view of an eagle's nest on the island. A set of stairs off the paved trail leads to an observation deck and to the upper trails along the abandoned railroad, which then lead to the lower trail network and back to the wetland complex.

REGULATIONS: Bikes, roller blades, skates, and other wheeled vehicles prohibited on the trails. Keep dogs leashed. No swimming, fishing, hunting, picking of plants, fires, camping, or overnight stays allowed.

HOURS: The trails are open daily, dawn to dusk. The nature center is open Monday–Friday, 9:00 AM–2:00 PM.

DIRECTIONS: From I-55, head east on IL 143 (exit 23) into Edwardsville. At the west end of town, turn south on M Street and go 4 blocks to Schiller Street. Turn left and proceed 3 blocks to the nature center on the right.

CONTACT INFORMATION: Watershed Nature Center, PO Box 843, Edwardsville, IL 62025; (618) 692-7578; www.edwpub.com/orgs/watershed

Southern Illinois

109. Eldon Hazlet State Park

HIGHLIGHTS:
- *Accessible trail*
- *Restored prairie*
- *Wildflowers*
- *Numerous bird species*
- *Various recreation facilities and sailboat harbor*

DESCRIPTION: Eldon Hazlet State Park is in Clinton County along the southwest shores of Lake Carlyle, the largest constructed lake in the state. With 3,000 acres, the park has numerous recreation facilities, the state's largest public campground, and over 7 miles of trails, a few of which are described here.

The **Bluestem Trail,** across from the administration building, is a .25-mile, accessible (packed gravel) trail that loops through a restored prairie. Along the trail may be seen an interpretive sign about birds of prey; over 50 species of native prairie plants, such as purple coneflower, rattlesnake master, and compass plant; and numerous butterflies and birds.

The **Cherokee Trail** consists of 3 loops totaling 3 miles. Each loop offers excellent views of the lake with portions going through some beautiful woods and ravines and past many wildflowers. Loop 1 connects with the **Youth Campground Trail** and goes over a few wooden bridges. Loop 3 leads to the pre–Civil War Burnside Cemetery, where some of Clinton County's original settlers are buried, and connects with the Pawnee Trail.

The **Eagle Trail** is a .75-mile loop near the Illini Campground that goes through a succession forest and past a restored prairie.

The **Kaskaskian Trail** (2.5 miles in length), across from the administration building, is named in honor of the Native Americans who inhabited the area around 900–1300. The trail goes through a succession forest and connects with the Pawnee Trail, the Eagle Trail, and the Osage Youth Group campground. Hiker signs and benches are found along the trail.

The **Pawnee Trail** goes through a succession field, along the lake, past Burnside Cemetery and the new park cabins, and connects with the Kaskaskian Trail, for a total distance of 1 mile.

The **Wetland Educational Trail,** the newest trail at the park, is a .25-mile, accessible, interpretive loop that goes by a small pond and a wetland and past various prairie plants. Six interpretive signs, a shelter,

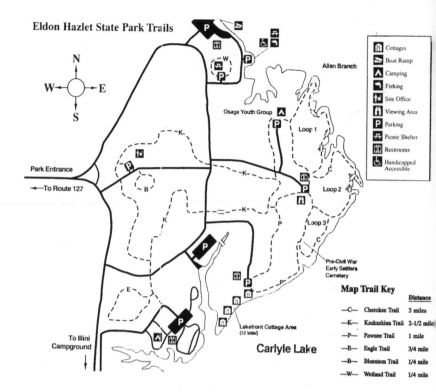

Eldon Hazlet State Park Trails

Allen Branch

Osage Youth Group

Loop 1

Park Entrance

To Route 127

Loop 2

Loop 3

Pre-Civil War
Early Settlers
Cemetery

Lakefront Cottage Area
(12 total)

To Illini
Campground

Carlyle Lake

	Cottages
	Boat Ramp
	Camping
	Fishing
	Site Office
	Viewing Area
	Parking
	Picnic Shelter
	Restrooms
	Handicapped Accessible

Map Trail Key

		Distance
—C—	Cherokee Trail	3 miles
—K—	Kaskaskian Trail	2-1/2 mile
—P—	Pawnee Trail	1 mile
—E—	Eagle Trail	3/4 mile
—B—	Bluestem Trail	1/4 mile
—W—	Wetland Trail	1/4 mile

and picnic tables are found along this packed gravel trail, and various shorebirds, wading birds, and other waterfowl may be seen.

Please note: Eldon Hazlet State Park has a population of eastern massasauga rattlesnakes. Watch out for these state-listed species, and report any sightings to park staff. In addition, there are steep drop-offs to the lake along some trail segments.

REGULATIONS: Leash all pets. Do not litter. Do not disturb wildlife. Bikes and horses prohibited on trails.

HOURS: The trails are open daily, except early November–mid-December during pheasant hunting season.

DIRECTIONS: From IL 127 north of Carlyle, turn east on Hazlet Park Road for 1.5 miles to 1860E. Turn left and travel 1.7 miles to the park entrance. The Bluestem and Kaskaskian Trails are across from the administration building. The Cherokee and Pawnee trailheads are reached by going past the administration building, turning left at the T, then taking a quick right and following the road to the end, where a large trail board is seen. To reach the Wetland Educational Trail, go left

194

at the first fork in the road within the park. Travel .7 mile to the second fork. Turn right at the sign for Apache Boat Access, go .3 mile, and turn left at the first unmarked road. Go .1 mile; parking is on the left.

CONTACT INFORMATION: Eldon Hazlet State Park, Carlyle, IL 62231; (618) 594-3015; www.dnr.state.il.us/lands/landmgt/parks/r4/eldon.htm

110. Carlyle Lake

HIGHLIGHTS:
- *Visitor center with various exhibits (plants, snakes, archaeology, construction of the lake), information, and gift shop*
- *Accessible, interpretive, and nature trails*
- *Campgrounds, swimming beach, picnic shelters, marina, and grills*
- *General Dean Suspension Bridge, listed on the National Register of Historic Places*

PROGRAMS AND EVENTS:
- *Weekly interpretive programs during summer months*
- *Arts and Ecology Series*
- *Dam tours (Memorial Day to Labor Day)*
- *Recreation Safety Festival*
- *Kaskaskia Duck Race*
- *Fireworks Spectacular*
- *Conservation Day*
- *Halloween Haunted Trail*
- *Christmastown Lighting Ceremony*
- *Sailing regattas*

DESCRIPTION: Carlyle Lake is the largest constructed body of water in Illinois at 26,000 acres in size. Around it there are many recreation facilities operated by the Corps of Engineers as well as the State of Illinois. The visitor center, swimming beach, marina, and a few nature and interpretive trails are near the dam at the south end of the lake, close to Carlyle in Clinton County. The historic General Dean Suspension Bridge below the dam is interesting to walk across. The bridge is the only one of its kind in the state and is listed on the National Register of Historic Places. In addition to the trails mentioned here, there are other recreation facilities and hiking trails on Carlyle Lake at Eldon Hazlet State Park and at South Shore State Park.

Willow Pond Nature Trail, outside the visitor center, is a short, fully accessible (concrete) interpretive trail that circles a small pond and goes past 2 overlooks and a shelter. It has 8 numbered posts corresponding to descriptions in the trail brochure. The trail is heavily wooded with sycamores, willows, maples, and cottonwoods.

Little Prairie Nature Trail, below the Carlyle Lake dam, is a .75-mile, wood-chip, interpretive trail heading through a fine bottomland forest and passing by a small restored prairie and creek. The trail has 12 numbered posts corresponding to descriptions in a trail brochure. Numerous bird species and mammals may be seen here. At times, the trail may be inundated or muddy.

The **Chipmunk Nature Trail,** on the east side of Carlyle Lake dam, is a .5-mile loop around the shores of the lake and down to the lake itself, where there are great views of the dam and the water. The trail winds through an oak-hickory forest and up and down a few small hills. Visitors may also walk or bicycle across Carlyle Lake Dam.

REGULATIONS: Stay on trails. Pack out all trash brought in. Leash all pets. Do not disturb wildlife.

HOURS: The visitor center is open daily, 10:00 AM–6:00 PM, Memorial Day to Labor Day, and Saturday and Sunday, Labor Day to Memorial Day.

DIRECTIONS: From US 50, turn north at Carlyle Lake Road (1430N) in Carlyle and proceed .6 mile to the visitor center parking area. From IL 127, turn east on Carlyle Lake Road (1430N), which is 1.2 miles north of the US 50/IL 127 junction in Carlyle, and proceed .6 mile to the visitor center. To reach the Little Prairie Nature Trail, proceed south from the visitor center for .4 mile, turn east at the West Spillway Picnic Area, and go .2 mile to the parking area on the south side of the road. To reach the Chipmunk Nature Trail, head east on US 50 past the dam to a sign for Dam East Access, turn left, and follow the signs to either the Lakeview Picnic Area or the McNair Group Area; the trail may be reached from both locations.

CONTACT INFORMATION: Carlyle Lake Project Office, 801 Lake Rd., Carlyle, IL 62231; Visitor Center: (618) 594-LAKE; Project Office: (618) 594-2484; www.mvs.usace.army.mil/carlyle

111. Cahokia Mounds State Historic Site

HIGHLIGHTS:
- *World Heritage Site*
- *2,000-acre prehistoric Mississippian city*
- *65 earthen mounds, including the largest prehistoric mound north of Mexico*
- *Interpretive center with exhibits, museum, and gift shop*
- *Interpretive trails*

PROGRAMS AND EVENTS:
- *Special educational programs*
- *Kids' Day*
- *Heritage America*
- *Nature/Cultural Hikes*
- *Artifact Identification Day*
- *Group tours*
- *Lectures*

DESCRIPTION: Cahokia Mounds State Historic Site in northern St. Clair County is a 2,000-acre Native American cultural site administered by the Illinois Historic Preservation Agency. On the site are more than 60 mounds built by people of the Mississippian culture from 1,100 to 700 years ago, including Monks Mound, which at over 100 feet high is the largest earthen mound north of Mexico. The interpretive center houses a site model, various murals, exhibit islands, a life-size diorama of Cahokia, an orientation film titled "City of the Sun," archaeology wells (sunken displays), a museum and gift shop, cafe area, and other visitor information. Various interpretive trail guide booklets may be purchased in the museum shop for the Twin Mounds/Plaza Tour, the Monks Mound/Stockade Tour, the Woodhenge/Mound 44 Tour, the Cahokia Mounds Nature/Cultural Hike (6 miles), and a short Prairie Nature Walk. An excellent way to experience the site is to take one of the nature/cultural hikes conducted a few times each year by archaeologists and botanists, who discuss the history of the site and point out the various plants and trees used by the original inhabitants. Also, self-guided tour tapes are available for loan at the information desk. A few of the shorter and more popular trails are described here.

The **Twin Mounds/Plaza Tour** takes the visitor from the interpretive building west towards a few of the mounds and the main Cahokia plaza, for a distance of 1 mile. Along the trail are red wooden markers corresponding to 6 trail descriptions. A small planted prairie area is crossed prior to the first stop. The trail goes over a ridge where a large stockade fence once surrounded Cahokia, past Twin Mounds, the central plaza, and various other smaller mounds. Directly north is Monks Mound.

The **Monks Mound/Stockade Tour** begins north of the visitor center and Collinsville Road, at the parking area for Monks Mound. This tour is .5 mile in length and includes 9 stops leading to the top of Monks Mound, a 100-foot climb most suitable for the physically fit. The trail also leads to a re-created stockade fence and a smaller mound. The 3 terraces of Monks Mound cover 14 acres and give an excellent view of the entire Cahokia village.

Further west, .5 mile down Collinsville Road, is a small parking area for the **Woodhenge/Mound 44 Tour.** The .5-mile tour passes by Woodhenge, a re-created sun calendar similar to what was used by the Mississippians, and Mound 44, an ancient platform mound.

To the southeast of the interpretive center is the 1-mile loop **Prairie State Nature Walk,** which takes the hiker past a restored prairie, a few small mounds, and a small wooded area. Some of the prairie plants that may be seen include Indian grass, big bluestem, butterfly weed, yellow coneflower, and purple coneflower. See the visitor desk for a map of this walk.

REGULATIONS: All items protected by law. No plant or artifact removal allowed. No flash photography permitted. Guide animals only allowed on grounds. No gum or writing materials (in the visitor center). Food and drink permitted only in cafeteria area and at picnic ground. Use stairway to climb Monks Mound. No climbing of any other mounds permitted.

HOURS: The interpretive center is open daily, 9:00 AM–5:00 PM. The site is open daily, 8:00 AM until dusk; closed New Year's Day, Dr. Martin Luther King Jr.'s Birthday, Presidents Day, Veterans Day, Thanksgiving Day, and Christmas Day.

DIRECTIONS: From I-55 southbound, head south on I-255 to Collinsville Road (exit 24), turn left, and proceed 1.5 miles to the site. From I-55 northbound, take IL 111 (exit 6) for .3 mile to Collinsville Road, turn left, and go 2 miles to the site.

CONTACT INFORMATION: Cahokia Mounds State Historic Site, 30 Ramey St., Collinsville, IL 62234; (618) 346-5610; www.state.il.us/hpa/sites/cahokiamounds.htm

112. Beall Woods State Park

HIGHLIGHTS:
- *Old growth forest—one of the largest untouched tracts east of the Mississippi*
- *Visitor center with photos, exhibits, wildlife, and nature games*
- *National Natural Landmark known as the "Forest of the Wabash"*
- *329-acre Illinois Nature Preserve*
- *Numerous bird and mammal species*
- *Wildflowers*
- *64 different tree species*
- *Interpretive and accessible trails*

PROGRAMS AND EVENTS:
- *Guided hikes*

DESCRIPTION: Beall Woods State Park in Wabash County is home to one of largest tracts of old growth forest east of the Mississippi River and features over 300 trees with trunk diameters greater than 30 inches at chest height. This 635 acres of upland and floodplain forest has been designated a National Natural Landmark as the "Forest of the Wabash." It also has 329 acres preserved under the Illinois Nature Preserves System. Sugar Creek and Coffee Creek flow through the park into the Wabash River. The new visitor center has photos of the large trees in the park, hands-on exhibits, and displays. Five interconnected trails totaling nearly 8 miles in length wind past the large trees and creeks and into the nature preserve, where numerous spring wildflowers may be found. The **Tulip Tree Trail** is an interpretive trail with 14 numbered stations corresponding to wildflower and tree descriptions in an associated trail guide. This trail loops through an upland forest paralleling Coffee Creek and makes a connection with the **Sweet Gum Trail.**

REGULATIONS: Stay on trail. All items protected by law. No collecting permitted. No pets, bicycles, or horses allowed on trails.

HOURS: The visitor center is open daily, 8:00 AM–4:00 PM. The park is open daily, daylight to 10:00 PM.

DIRECTIONS: From IL 15 in Mt. Carmel, take IL 1 south to Keensburg. From I-64, turn north on IL 1 (exit 130) and travel 11 miles to

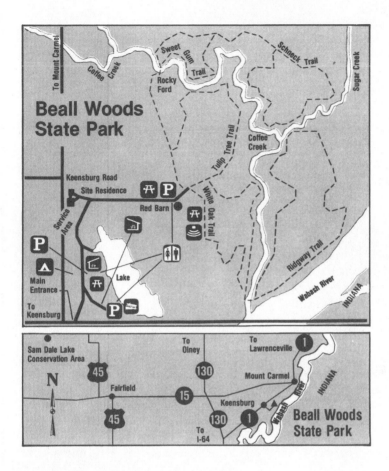

Keensburg. Following the signs in Keensburg, go east for 2 miles to the park.

CONTACT INFORMATION: Beall Woods State Park, 9285 Beall Woods Ave., Mt. Carmel, IL 62863; Park Office: (618) 298-2442; Visitor Center: (618) 298-2441; www.dnr.state.il.us/lands/landmgt/parks/r5/beall.htm

113. Cedarhurst

HIGHLIGHTS:
- *Cedarhurst Art Center*
- *Mitchell Museum and Children's Gallery*
- *Gift shop*
- *Sculpture garden*
- *Nature and braille trails*
- *Bird sanctuary*
- Cedarhurst Quarterly *newsletter*

PROGRAMS AND EVENTS:
- *Cedarhurst Art and Craft Fair*
- *Concert series*
- *Art classes and workshops in weaving, basketry, pottery, painting, drawing, stained glass, carving, and photography*

DESCRIPTION: Cedarhurst is a unique facility combining art and nature in Mt. Vernon (Jefferson County). The 85-acre grounds feature the Mitchell Museum and gift shop, a sculpture garden, Cedarhurst Art Center, a nature trail, and a braille trail. The museum offers art exhibits and a children's gallery, while the Cedarhurst Art Center holds various classes and programs. A large craft fair is held there on the first weekend after Labor Day, and many art and concert programs are also sponsored. Two trails are on the grounds.

The **Juniper Ridge Nature Trail,** north of the museum, may be started between the 2 ponds or to the west of the second pond. This trail takes the visitor to a small wooded area where there are 2 loops. A bird sanctuary on the northern loop features photos of birds and animals, and the trail continues with a connecting spur to the Cedarhurst Art Center. The other loop goes through a small wooded tract and parallels the ponds for a short distance. The **Braille Trail** is a short wooded path east of the museum that has guide ropes along the trail as well as braille signs. At press time, there was some uncertainty whether it would remain open in the future.

REGULATIONS: Stay on trails.

HOURS: The grounds and the Mitchell Museum are open Tuesday–Saturday, 10:00 AM–5:00 PM; and Sunday, 1:00–5:00 PM.

From I-64/57 in Mt. Vernon, head east on IL 15 (exit 95) for 2 miles to 27th Street, where a sign will be seen for the Mitchell Museum. Turn north on 27th, go 7 blocks to Richview Road, and head east a few blocks to the entrance on the north side of the road.

CONTACT INFORMATION: Cedarhurst, PO Box 923, Mt. Vernon, IL 62864; (618) 242-1236; www.cedarhurst.org

114. Rend Lake

HIGHLIGHTS:

- *18,000-acre lake*
- *21,000 acres of public lands*
- *Visitor center with exhibits (on animals, fish, and Native Americans), bookstore, and general information*
- *Nature and interpretive trails*
- *Blue heron nesting sites*
- *Wildlife viewing decks*
- *Public beach, marina, campground, and picnic areas*

PROGRAMS AND EVENTS:

- *Environmental Science Programs (e.g., Remarkable Reptiles, Which Fish Is It?, Art of Beekeeping, Wildlife Watching, Babes in the Woods, Taste of Freedom Festival, Living Puppets, Nocturnal Mammals, Kids' Fun Day, Beach Blast, Stream Critters, Illiniwek Connections, Archaeology of Rend Lake, Tigers of the Sky, Goodness Snakes, Common Critters of the Rend Lake Area, The Predators, Raptors)*
- *Evening Campfire Program*
- *Beach Program*
- *Earth Day*
- *Youth Conservation Education Camp*
- *Family Fishing Derby*
- *Summer Beach Blast*
- *The Rend Lake Cleanup*
- *Watchable Wildlife of Rend Lake*
- *Introduction to Rend Lake*
- *Wildlife Management Techniques*
- *Hunter and boating safety classes*
- *Summer Sunset Series (music)*
- *Taste of Freedom*
- *Festival of Arts and Crafts*

DESCRIPTION: The Rend Lake complex, in Jefferson and Franklin counties in south central Illinois, consists of an 18,000-acre lake and 21,000 acres of public recreation lands surrounding it. Built by the Corps of Engineers in 1972 to provide flood control in the Big Muddy River basin and for recreation opportunities, the complex offers camp-

Information kiosk at trailhead of Blackberry Nature Trail, Rend Lake

ing, picnicking, swimming, boating, and wildlife viewing opportunities, as does Wayne Fitzgerrell State Park and lodge. A visitor center on the east side of the dam offers general information and exhibits on natural resources and archaeology. A wetland and wildflower demonstration garden may be found behind the visitor center. A few nature and interpretive trails around Rend Lake are described here, including one at Rend Lake College.

The **Blackberry Nature Trail** is an interpretive trail with 14 numbered posts in an oak-hickory forest. An A-frame trail board at the trailhead has information on plants and animals found in the area, a trail map, and a map of the lake. A brochure is available that describes many of the trees found along the trail.

The **Green Heron Pond Trail** is in the South Marcum Recreation Area campground. This .25-mile trail takes visitors around Heron Pond, offering numerous bird-watching and fishing opportunities.

The **Gun Creek Wetland/South** area is on top of a levee and allows visitors a chance to observe wildlife in an impounded wetland. This .25-mile trail leads to an accessible platform for viewing wildlife.

The **Rend Lake College Prairie Trail** at the Rend Lake College campus, a 1.5-mile trail system, makes its way through a 40-acre restored prairie, part of the Rend Lake Prairie Restoration Project carried out by the school. The old Independence School sits at the trailhead. The trail system consists of 3 loops with typical street signs identifying the trail. Look for big bluestem, black-eyed susan, purple coneflower, and other plants while hiking.

REGULATIONS: Stay on trail.

HOURS: The site is open only during daylight for safety.

DIRECTIONS: From I-57, go west on IL 14 (exit 71) for 2.6 miles to Rend City Road (900E). Turn north and go 3 miles to 1190N. Turn east and go 2.8 miles to the visitor center. To reach Green Heron Pond Trail, continue past the visitor center to the center of the campground at the South Marcum Recreation Area. To reach Blackberry Nature Trail from IL 14, take Rend Lake Road for 4.9 miles to the trailhead on the right side of the road. To reach Gun Creek Wetland/South, take I-57 to Ina (exit 83). Head east on 175N, turn south on 1400E, then east on 1800N, and travel a short distance to the parking area on the south side of the road, right past Gun Creek. To reach Rend Lake College Prairie Trail, take I-57 to the Ina exit (exit 83) and head west on this road for 1.7 miles to the college parking lot. The trail is on the north side of the road.

CONTACT INFORMATION: Rend Lake Management Office, 12220 Rend City Rd., Benton, IL 62812; (618) 724-2493; www.mvs.usace.army.mil/rend

Rend Lake College, 468 N. Ken Gray Parkway, Ina, IL 62846; (618) 437-5321, ext. 247

115. Piney Creek Ravine Nature Preserve

HIGHLIGHTS:
- *111-acre Illinois Nature Preserve*
- *Ravine and canyon*
- *Shortleaf pines*
- *Bluffs*
- *Petroglyphs*

DESCRIPTION: Piney Creek Nature Preserve in Randolph County is protected as an Illinois Nature Preserve for its ravine and canyon, bluffs, and unusual plants. A 2.4-mile loop trail winds around the nearly 200-acre site through a wooded upland of oaks and hickories and down to the Piney Creek Ravine, where beautiful sandstone rock outcrops, bluffs, and waterfalls are encountered. It continues through the canyon (watch your footing and keep an eye on children), past sandstone cliffs, and along Piney Creek. Near the end of the canyon, set into the cliffs on the right side of the creek, is a protected petroglyph site. The trail then makes its way to the top of the canyon and loops back down to the start.

REGULATIONS: No hunting, camping, alcohol, or littering permitted. Leash pets.

HOURS: The preserve is open only during daylight for safety.

DIRECTIONS: From the IL 3/151 junction in Jackson County, travel 7.3 miles northwest on IL 3 to Hog Hill Road. Turn north on Hog Hill Road and travel 5 miles until a sign is seen for the nature preserve. Turn left on this road and travel 1.4 miles to the parking area on the right side of the road.

CONTACT INFORMATION: Piney Creek Ravine Nature Preserve, 4301 S. Lakeside Dr., Chester, IL 62033; (618) 826-2706

116.   Green Earth I

HIGHLIGHTS:
- *Interpretive trail*
- *Wooded tract*
- *Wildflowers*

DESCRIPTION: Green Earth I in Carbondale (Jackson County) is a hilly, wooded, 23-acre tract on the outskirts of the campus of Southern Illinois University. Owned and managed by Green Earth, Inc., a nonprofit land trust, and open to the public, the area consists of an upland forest, a succession area, and a bottomland forest. The **Herbie Beyler Trail** is a 1-mile loop with numbered posts that correspond to descriptions in a trail brochure available at the trailhead or by writing to Green Earth, Inc. In addition, there are paint blazes on trees to help guide visitors. The trail features numerous wildflowers such as mayapple, some large maple trees, a small pond, and many bird species that make their home here.

REGULATIONS: No hunting allowed.

HOURS: The site is open daily, dawn to dusk.

Herbie Beyler trailhead, Green Earth I

DIRECTIONS: From IL 13 in Carbondale, turn south at South Lewis Street (first street west of the mall) and travel .9 mile to East Park Street. Turn left and go 3 blocks to the parking area on the right, where there is a sign for Green Earth I.

CONTACT INFORMATION: Green Earth, Inc., PO Box 441, Carbondale, IL 62903; www.globaleyes.net/Community/GreenEarth/index.html

117.   Little Grand Canyon

HIGHLIGHTS:
- *Unusual ecological area*
- *Outstanding rock features, cliffs, shelter bluffs, ledges, and seasonal waterfalls*
- *Overlooks to the Big Muddy River*
- *National Natural Landmark*

DESCRIPTION: The Little Grand Canyon in Jackson County has one of the most dramatic trails in the Shawnee National Forest, a challenging, 3.6-mile loop that begins and ends on a hilltop with strenuous climbs up and down 2 rock ravines. The trail is partly paved from the parking area heading either north or west along the ridge line above the

Trail leading down sandstone creek bed into canyon, Little Grand Canyon

ravine. It then turns to dirt and natural rock in the waterfall and ravine areas. Scenic overlooks are found at each end of the ravine, with the Big Muddy overlook at the west end having a more spectacular view of the floodplain and of Swallow Rock Bluff. There are interpretive signs in the parking area as well as at the Big Muddy overlook, and spray-painted white diamonds on rocks and trees mark the trail. The trail descends down the ridge line on each segment and into rock-lined ravines that can be quite slippery and have drops of a few feet. At the bottom of each ravine, the trail follows the floodplain and the bluff line. Large cottonwoods, sycamores, oaks, and some intermittent waterfalls may be seen along this segment, as well as numerous shelter bluffs. As this is a rocky trail, watch your footing and hang on to children. Poisonous snakes also inhabit the area, and flash floods have been known to occur in the floodplain.

REGULATIONS: Stay on trail. Do not litter.

HOURS: The site is open daily, 7:00 AM–10:00 PM.

DIRECTIONS: From IL 127, travel south out of Murphysboro for 5.7 miles to Etherton Road, where a sign is seen for Little Grand Canyon. Follow Etherton Road west for 2.5 miles to Poplar Ridge Road. Turn left and travel 3.7 miles to the turnoff and parking area.

CONTACT INFORMATION: Murphysboro Ranger District, 2221 Walnut St., Murphysboro, IL 62966; (618) 687-1731; TTY (618) 687-1726; www.fs.fed.us/r9/shawnee

118. William Marberry Arboretum

HIGHLIGHTS:
- *24-acre arboretum*
- *Pine plantation*
- *Holly collection*
- *Pond with bald cypresses*
- *Oak stand*
- *Interpretive trail*

DESCRIPTION: William Marberry Arboretum, at the south end of Carbondale in Jackson County near the campus of Southern Illinois University, is 24 acres with over 20,000 trees, a pond, and a 1.5-mile interpretive trail. William Marberry, a former employee of the university for whom the park is named, traveled the world extensively during World War II and brought back many unusual tree seedlings, including some oriental species such as spring cherry. A plantation of large ponderosa pines as well as a forest of oak, hickory, and bald cypress may be seen while hiking the dirt and wood-chip trail. There are 9 numbered wooden posts that correspond to descriptions of the features of the site in a trail brochure available from the Carbondale Park District.

REGULATIONS: No bikes or motorcycles allowed. Leash dogs.

HOURS: The park is open daily, 6:00 AM–10:00 PM.

DIRECTIONS: From IL 13 in Carbondale, turn south on South Wall Street for 2 miles to the T at Pleasant Hill Road. Proceed straight ahead into the parking area. From US 51, go east on Pleasant Hill Road and proceed .6 mile to the entrance on the right side of the road.

CONTACT INFORMATION: Carbondale Park District, 1115 W. Sycamore, PO Box 1326, Carbondale, IL 62903-1326; (618) 529-9364

119. Oakwood Bottoms Greentree Reservoir

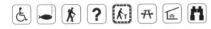

HIGHLIGHTS:
- *Pin oak forest*
- *Accessible trails and fishing piers*
- *Bird-watching and animal observation areas*

DESCRIPTION: Oakwood Bottoms Greentree Reservoir, along the Big Muddy River in Jackson County and operated by the Shawnee National Forest, provides habitat for migrating and wintering waterfowl and a laboratory for studying the effects of floodwater on a forest of pin oaks. The site is comprised of a series of levies, pump stations, and impoundments that get flooded in the winter months to attract the migrating waterfowl. This interpretive and accessible site features 2 nature trails, a pond, and accessible shelters, fishing piers, and rest rooms.

The **Walk of Life Trail** is a .25-mile loop on a boardwalk with interpretive signs. Beginning east of the parking area, this accessible trail goes through one of the flooded timber impoundments. The **Lake Trail** loops around the small pond for .5 mile on a mowed grass path with rest benches and fishing piers. Numerous bird species may be seen while hiking these trails, such as wood ducks, great blue herons, belted king-

Walk of Life trailhead, Oakwood Bottoms Greentree Reservoir

fishers, and woodpeckers. Poisonous snakes also make their home here, so exercise caution.

REGULATIONS: No camping allowed. Use trash cans.

HOURS: The site is open only during daylight for safety.

DIRECTIONS: From IL 3, head 5 miles south of the junction with IL 149 to Johns Spur Road. Turn east and travel 1 mile, going over the railroad tracks, to the parking area on the left side of the road.

CONTACT INFORMATION: Murphysboro Ranger District, 2221 Walnut St., Murphysboro, IL 62966; (618) 687-1731; TTY (618) 687-1726; www.fs.fed.us/r9/shawnee

120. Pomona Natural Bridge

HIGHLIGHTS:
- *Natural sandstone bridge*
- *Other rock formations*
- *Mature oak, hickory, and beech forest*

DESCRIPTION: No visit to the Shawnee National Forest is complete without a trip to Pomona Natural Bridge, a recreation site near the town of Pomona in Jackson County. This natural sandstone bridge is an impressive 90 feet across and 25 feet above the creek bottom and is surrounded by a mature oak, hickory, and beech forest, the ravine, and other rock outcrops in the area. A .3-mile loop trail on gravel, dirt, and rock leads to the natural bridge, with a segment going over it. A sign at the trailhead describes how the forces of erosion carved out this natural arch. An overlook encountered prior to reaching the arch makes a great stop for some photo opportunities, while a bench on another trail segment offers a good view of the arch when the leaves are off the trees. There are many steep descents here, and the rocks can become quite slippery; poisonous snakes also inhabit the area, including the timber rattlesnake. For a longer hike, the **Cedar Lake Trail** may be found nearby, on the east side of IL 127.

View of stone arch, Pomona Natural Bridge

REGULATIONS: Stay on trail. Pick up litter.

HOURS: The site is open year-round.

DIRECTIONS: From IL 127, head south out of Murphysboro for 10 miles to Pomona Road. Turn west and travel .7 mile into Pomona. Turn right at Sadler Road, passing the Pomona General Store, and travel 1 block to Bridge Road (gravel). Follow it straight for 2.2 miles to the parking area.

CONTACT INFORMATION: Murphysboro Ranger District, 2221 Walnut St., Murphysboro, IL 62966; (618) 687-1731 or TTY (618) 687-1726; www.fs.fed.us/r9/shawnee

121. Touch of Nature Environmental Center

HIGHLIGHTS:
- *Interpretive trail with 20 stations*
- *Wildflowers*
- *Pond*

DESCRIPTION: Touch of Nature Environmental Center, in Jackson County along Little Grassy Lake near Carbondale and next to Giant City State Park, is a 3,100-acre camp operated by Southern Illinois University where many outdoor-related courses are held throughout the year. Parts of the interpretive loop **Woodland World Trail** consist of an old road-bed, and there are 20 numbered wooden posts corresponding to descriptions in a trail brochure available from Touch of Nature. The trail begins next to the pond, then makes its way through a succession forest, goes over some small hills and valleys, passes by a building used for Touch of Nature programs, and comes back to the pond.

REGULATIONS: A permit is required to fish in the pond.

HOURS: The trail is open only during daylight for safety.

DIRECTIONS: From IL 13 in Carbondale, go south on Giant City Road for 11 miles to the entrance for Touch of Nature on the east side of the road. Follow the entrance road for .9 mile, staying to the right all the time, to a pond on the left side of the road. Near the pond is a sign for the trail.

CONTACT INFORMATION: Touch of Nature Environmental Center, Mail-code 6888, Southern Illinois University, Carbondale, IL 62901-6888; (618) 453-1121; www.pso.siu.edu/tonec

122.   Giant City State Park

HIGHLIGHTS:
- *"Giant City" rock features*
- *National Natural Landmark*
- *3,900-acre wooded park*
- *Sandstone bluffs, shelter bluffs, and rock formations*
- *Visitor center with park map, audiotape, books, exhibits, and children's corner*
- *Lodge, cabins, and restaurant*
- *Water tower with observation deck*
- *Restored prairies*
- *Wildflowers*
- *75 tree species*
- *Ferns and mosses*
- *170-acre Fern Rocks Nature Preserve*
- *Native American stone wall*
- *Nature and interpretive trails, backpacking trails, and horse trails*

PROGRAMS AND EVENTS:
- *School and youth group programs (e.g., Trees of Giant City, Birds of Giant City, Mammals of Giant City, Where's the Water at Giant City, Spring Woodland Wildflowers, Fall Colors, Winter Tracking)*
- *Wandering among the Woodland Wildflowers*
- *Mothers and Flowers*
- *Fathers in the Woods*
- *Summertime at Giant City*
- *Leaf, Bark, and Seed Hikes — The Trees of Giant City*

DESCRIPTION: Giant City State Park is generally regarded as one of the most beautiful parks in Illinois. This 3,900-acre site straddling Jackson and Union counties has numerous recreation facilities and is known for its sandstone bluffs, shelter bluffs, and "giant city streets" through towering rock formations. The area was occupied around 600–1200 AD by Native Americans referred to by archaeologists as the Woodland people. Clues that they lived in the area may be seen on the Stone Fort Trail, where there are remnants of a rock wall on top of a bluff, and on the Indian Creek Trail, where there are pieces of chert in the shelter bluff. There is a wide diversity of flora and fauna in the park, and there are

218

many large oaks and hickories, successional fields, restored prairies, and wildflowers. Among the features are a large campground at the east end of the park; a lodge and cabins built by the Civilian Conservation Corps (1936) that are available for overnight lodging; a horse stable for horseback riding; a pond for fishing; and a boat launch near the campground that allows visitors to explore Little Grassy Lake as well as Crab Orchard Wilderness Area. Touch of Nature Environmental Center also borders Giant City State Park. In addition to the nature trails described here, there are horse trails, the **Red Cedar Backpack Trail,** and a portion of the **River-to-River Backpack Trail.** Brochures are available for these trails at the visitor center.

The **Arrow-Wood Self-Interpretive Nature Trail,** at the south end of the visitor center parking lot where a trail board is seen, is the newest trail in the park. It is a .3 mile in length on a wood-chip and gravel surface and goes through a restored prairie and then loops through a successional forest. Trail signs identify the various shrub and tree species along the trail and the uses made of the wood, particularly by Native Americans.

The **Devil's Standtable Nature Trail** is across from shelter 2 and takes the visitor past some unique rock formations and bluffs, including a shelter bluff. The interesting mushroom-shaped rock known as the "standtable" was one of the reasons the property was purchased for a park. The trail is .3 mile long on a wood-chip and dirt path.

Giant City Nature Trail, near shelter 3, allows the visitor to experience the "streets" of Giant City on a 1-mile dirt path among towering rock walls and canyons and to be awed by the massive erosional forces that created them. Shelter bluffs, the Balanced Rock formation, and a narrow passage referred to as Fat Man's Squeeze are also found along this trail through an oak-hickory forest. Wildflowers may be seen in the spring and early summer, and there are numbered posts along the trail corresponding to descriptions in the trail brochure of the trees, bluffs, rock formations, and culture of the Woodland people.

East of the visitor center, the .75-mile **Indian Creek Nature Trail** goes through an oak-hickory forest, over Indian Creek, and to a small shelter bluff facing south that was once occupied by Native Americans. Small chert flakes may still be found in the drip line of the shelter. The path is composed of wood chips, and 2 new, wooden bridges go over Indian Creek.

The **Post Oak Nature Trail** is a .3-mile, paved, accessible path that winds its way on a bluff to a boardwalk over a pond, into the forest, and along the edge of the bluff line where there are viewing platforms. Rest rooms and a trail board may be found at the trailhead, and there are benches on the trail. Fishing is allowed in the pond.

The **Stone Fort Nature Trail** is a .3-mile loop to the top of a sandstone bluff where a rebuilt stone wall may be seen. About 5 feet tall and

Balanced Rock seen on the Giant City Nature Trail, Giant City State Park

265 feet long and constructed of rocks brought up from the creek near the parking lot, the wall once possibly served as a defensive barrier for the Woodland people. Also on top of the bluff is the site of the Lewis Village, which was home to possibly 25 to 50 Native Americans. The trail skirts the edge of the bluff line and offers good views of the valley below.

The **Trillium Trail** is a 2-mile loop through an outstanding ecological area within a 160-acre, protected Illinois Nature Preserve (Fern Rocks), known for its unique plants and geology. The trail takes visitors along the bottom of a bluff past numerous rock features, caves, waterfalls (seasonal), and shelter bluffs. After paralleling Stonefort Creek for a short distance, it climbs to the top of the bluff where, when the foliage is off the trees, good views of the surrounding terrain may be had. The trail is marked with numbered posts corresponding to descriptions in the trail brochure of the flora and fauna as well as the geology of the site. Numerous wildflowers and other plant species seen here include the state-endangered white flower mint and the grove bluegrass, as well as French's shooting star, trillium, and mayapple.

Please note: Many hazardous areas exist within the park, including high bluffs, rocks, slippery trail surfaces, steep grades, creek crossings, wooden stairs, and other hazards. Exercise caution throughout the park, especially with children.

REGULATIONS: Leash all pets. Stay on trails. No alcohol permitted from September 1 to May 31. No food allowed on trails. All natural and historic features protected by law.

HOURS: The park is open daily, 6:00 AM–10:00 PM. The visitor center is open daily, 8:00 AM–4:00 PM.

DIRECTIONS: From IL 13 at the east end of Carbondale, turn south on Giant City Road and travel 13 miles into the park.

CONTACT INFORMATION: Giant City State Park, 336 S. Church Rd., Makanda, IL 62958; (618) 457-4836; www.dnr.state.il.us/lands/landmgt/parks/r5/gc.htm

123. Crab Orchard National Wildlife Refuge

HIGHLIGHTS:

- *Visitor center with various exhibits, books, and permits*
- *Accessible trail*
- *43,000-acre wildlife refuge and 4,000-acre wilderness*
- *Reconstructed schoolhouse*
- *Pine woodland*
- *Bird-watching area with over 200 songbird species*
- *Restored prairie*
- *Sandstone waterfall (seasonal)*
- *Shelter bluffs and rock formations*
- *Wildflowers*
- *Hardwood forest*
- *Interpretive trail signs*

PROGRAMS AND EVENTS:

- *Discovery self-guided refuge tours (Sundays in October)*
- *Bald eagle viewing (January)*
- *Cemetery tours*
- *Spring wildflower tours*

DESCRIPTION: The Crab Orchard visitor center is the gateway to the 43,000-acre Crab Orchard National Wildlife Refuge and Wilderness Area in Williamson County. The visitor center has general refuge information, permits, rest rooms, water, books, and various exhibits. South of the visitor center, along IL 148, is a wildlife observation stand overlooking a portion of the refuge.

The **Woodland Nature Trail** begins outside the visitor center at the east end of the parking area. This .25-mile, paved accessible trail leads down to a pond where there is a wooden fishing pier. At the trailhead and along the trail are braille markers, as well as a bench.

The **Chamnesstown School Trail** is just west of the visitor center; there is a trail board at the trailhead. Just east of the trailhead is a restored schoolhouse that dates from 1860 and was rebuilt in 1976. The 1-mile trail makes a loop through a pine forest and past 2 small ponds. A short trail spur near the start leads to a bird-watching area, and another spur cuts across the loop, shortening the trail's length.

The scenic **Rocky Bluff Trail** is in the southern part of the refuge near Devils Kitchen Lake. The trailhead may be found .8 mile southeast of the boat dock. The trail is a loop and goes counterclockwise, following the

View of seasonal waterfall on Rocky Bluff Trail, Crab Orchard National Wildlife Refuge

trail markers, as it winds through an oak-hickory upland forest and down to Grassy Creek. Along the way there are numerous wildflowers such as trout lily and mayapple, ferns, wildlife, and interesting rock formations that include shelter bluffs and a waterfall. White arrows at a few trail junctions lead the hiker along, and there are 7 informational signs describing the flora and fauna found in the area. The trail also joins the **Wild Turkey Trail** for a short distance.

Please note: The Rocky Bluff Trail has some challenging climbs, bluffs, slippery rock surfaces, and other hazards. Exercise caution, especially with children. All vehicles must display a refuge permit, which may be purchased at the main visitor center or at the Devils Kitchen boat dock.

REGULATIONS: User fees and permits (obtainable at the main visitor center or at the Devils Kitchen Lake boat dock) are required of all vehicles and boats using the refuge, including the parking area for the Rocky Bluff Trail. Foot traffic only allowed on trails. Stay on trail.

HOURS: The visitor center is open daily, 8:00 AM–5:00 PM. Trails are open only during daylight for safety.

DIRECTIONS: From IL 13 west of Marion, turn south on IL 148, and proceed 1.7 miles to the visitor center on the east side of the road. From I-57, take IL 148 west (exit 45) for 8.2 miles to the visitor center. The trailhead for the Chamnesstown School Trail is .4 mile west of the visitor center, on the north side of Pigeon Creek Road. To reach the Rocky Bluff trailhead, near the Devils Kitchen Lake boat dock, continue south on IL 148 for 5 miles to Little Grassy Road. Turn west and go 2 miles to South Wolf Creek Road. Turn south and go 2 miles to

200N (Lake Tacoma Road). Head west, following the curve into the Devils Kitchen Lake area, and go 3.5 miles to the trailhead on the right. From I-57, take IL 148 west (exit 45) for 7 miles to Little Grassy Road. Turn west (left) on Little Grassy Road and follow the directions above.

CONTACT INFORMATION: Crab Orchard National Wildlife Refuge, 8588 Route 148, Marion, IL 62959; (618) 997-3344; midwest.fws.gov/craborchard

124. Garden of the Gods Recreation Area

HIGHLIGHTS:
- *Natural sandstone features*
- *Rock formations (Camel Rock, Table Rock, Anvil Rock, Devil's Smokestack)*
- *Unique geology*
- *Views of wilderness area and Shawnee Hills*
- *Observation and interpretive trail*
- *Connection to the River-to-River Trail*

DESCRIPTION: Garden of the Gods Recreation Area, in the southeast corner of Saline County and the eastern reaches of the Shawnee National Forest, includes a picnic area and campground, a backpacker's parking lot, and access to the **River-to-River Trail** and the Garden of the Gods Wilderness. A good starting point for scenic views is the .25-mile **Garden of the Gods Observation Trail.** A large trail board at the trailhead explains the natural history and geology of the area. The partially accessible trail leads to some interesting rock formations such as Table Rock and Devil's Smokestack and to observation points looking out over the Shawnee Hills. Interpretive signs along the trail describe the geology of the wilderness area. Connecting trails lead to the River-to-River Trail, and other trails begin near the picnic area and campground.

REGULATIONS: No bikes allowed on trails. Keep all pets on a leash. Use trash receptacles. Camp only in designated sites. Disposable food and beverage containers are not permitted on the observation trail.

HOURS: The site is open daily, 6:00 AM–10:00 PM.

DIRECTIONS: From IL 13 in Harrisburg, go south on IL 34 past Herod to Karbers Ridge Blacktop. Turn east (left) and go 3 miles to County Highway 10. Turn left and follow the signs to the parking area.

CONTACT INFORMATION: Elizabeth Ranger District, RR 2 Box 4, Elizabethtown, IL 62931; (618) 287-2201; www.fs.fed.us/r9/shawnee

GARDEN OF THE GODS RECREATION AREA

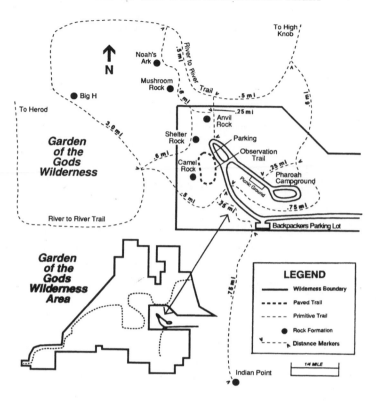

125.   Rim Rock

HIGHLIGHTS:
- *Native American rock wall*
- *Sandstone cliffs and rock formations*
- *Pounds Hollow vista*
- *Ox-Lot Cave shelter bluff*
- *Partly accessible trail*
- *Sandstone barrens*
- *National Recreation Trail*

DESCRIPTION: Rim Rock, in Gallatin County within the Shawnee National Forest and part of the Rim Rock/Pounds Hollow Recreation Complex, is a 50-acre isolated bluff. The **Rim Rock National Recreation Trail** loops for .75 mile on top of the bluff. At the base of the bluff, it intersects the **Beaver Trail,** which leads north to the Pounds Hollow Lake Recreation Area, where there is a campground and a swimming beach. The trailheads to the Rim Rock Trail as well as the Beaver Trail may be found at the parking area.

A trail board for the Rim Rock Trail includes information on the natural history of the area, the role of the Civilian Conservation Corps in the development of the site, a description of the Native Americans who once occupied the area, and a trail map. Five other interpretive signs are also seen along the trail, which passes by a Native American rock wall, through a red cedar plantation, to a vista of Pounds Hollow Lake, and then down to an observation platform and a set of stairs. The trail is partly accessible to the observation platform by going to the left. There is a narrow passageway called Fat Man's Misery on the stairs leading down to the base of the bluff, where interesting rock walls and formations may be seen. The trail then leads to the Ox-Lot Cave, a shelter bluff, where a trail sign explains that settlers used to keep their oxen and horses within a fenced area under this shelter. Good views of the sandstone bluff are found in this lower area, and from here it is possible to take the Beaver Trail around the bluff and over to Pounds Hollow Lake or follow it back to the parking area; alternatively, the visitor may go back up the stairs and continue on the loop of the Rim Rock Trail past some interesting vistas, sandstone barrens, and the rock wall before returning to the parking area.

REGULATIONS: No camping allowed. Stay on trail.

Ox-Lot Cave,
Rim Rock

HOURS: The site is open daily, 6:00 AM–10:00 PM.

DIRECTIONS: From IL 13 west of Shawneetown, turn south on IL 1 for 8.5 miles to Pounds Hollow Road. Turn west and go 3 miles until a sign is seen for the Rim Rock Trail. Turn north and go a short distance to the parking area.

CONTACT INFORMATION: Elizabethtown Ranger District, RR 2 Box 4, Elizabethtown, IL 62931; (618) 287-2201; www.fs.fed.us/r9/shawnee

126. Quetil Trail

HIGHLIGHTS:
- *Interpretive trail*
- *Sandstone rock bluffs and other rock features*
- *Rail-to-trail conversion*
- *View of Bald Knob Cross*

DESCRIPTION: The Quetil Trail in historic Alto Pass (Union County) was converted from an abandoned track of the old Cairo and St. Louis Narrow Gauge Railroad and is named after Charles Julius Quetil. This .5-mile (one-way) trail follows a dry upland community along a sandstone bluff line on one side, with boulders and a moist soil forest on the other. Geologists refer to this sandstone as Battery Rock. The trail has 2 signs explaining the flora and geology of the area; one of the signs is mounted inside the old railroad switch box. At the trailhead is a trail board, and there are benches along the trail. A set of stairs lead up to the top of the bluffs, where there is a striking view of Bald Knob Cross and the Bald Knob Cross Wilderness Area. The end of the trail is marked with a private property sign.

Trailhead and interpretive signs, Quetil Trail

REGULATIONS: No horses, alcohol, climbing, or picking flowers permitted.

HOURS: The trail closes at dark.

DIRECTIONS: From IL 127, travel south out of Murphysboro about 13 miles to Alto Pass, turn east on Alto Pass Road (Main Street), and go .4 mile to the trailhead and parking area.

CONTACT INFORMATION: (800) 248-4373

127.   Lincoln Memorial Picnic Grounds

HIGHLIGHTS:
- *Accessible trail*
- *Site of Lincoln-Douglas debate*
- *Home of Jonesboro Ranger Station*
- *Fishing pond*

DESCRIPTION: The Lincoln Memorial Picnic Grounds, in Jonesboro (Union County), is the home of the Jonesboro Ranger Station and the site of the Lincoln-Douglas debate in 1858. The site includes picnic facilities in tranquil surroundings as well as the **Lincoln Memorial Trail.** The trail consists of 3 paved loops (an outside loop, a pond loop, and an inside loop) that wind for 1 mile around the property, circling a small fishing pond and crossing it on a small wooden bridge (with steps).

REGULATIONS: No motorized vehicles allowed on trail.

HOURS: The site is open daily, 8:00 AM–10:00 PM. The ranger station is open Monday–Friday, 8:00 AM–4:30 PM.

Fishing in pond, Lincoln Memorial Picnic Grounds

231

DIRECTIONS: From the junction of IL 127 and IL 146 in Jonesboro's town square, go 3 blocks north on Main Street to the parking area for the picnic grounds on the west side of IL 127.

CONTACT INFORMATION: Jonesboro Ranger District, 521 N. Main St., Jonesboro, IL 62952; (618) 833-8576; www.fs.fed.us/r9/shawnee

128.   Ferne Clyffe State Park

HIGHLIGHTS:
- *Waterfalls*
- *Sandstone bluffs, cliffs, and rock formations*
- *Diverse wildlife and over 700 species of plants,*
  including ferns and wildflowers
- *53-acre Round Bluff Nature Preserve*
- *Hawk's Cave*
- *River-to-River Backpack Trail*
- *Interpretive and nature trails*

DESCRIPTION: Ferne Clyffe State Park in Johnson and Union Counties is a 2,400-acre site nestled in the hills of the Shawnee National Forest, with impressive sandstone bluffs, rock formations, shelter bluffs, creeks, and a great variety of plants and wildlife. The park features the Round Bluff Nature Preserve and a part of the **River-to-River Trail,** and there are 17 other trails both within the main park as well as at the nearby Cedar Bluff and Draper Bluff tracts. Wildflowers abound within the park, especially along the trail at the nature preserve, and there are outstanding rock formations and views at Hawk's Cave, the waterfall, and the bluffs at the preserve. In the fall, the foliage around the park and the park lake is spectacular. A few of the interpretive and nature trails are described here.

The **Big Rocky Hollow Trail** is a level, .75-mile path that leads to an impressive, if seasonal, waterfall, with a view of cliffs on the left side and a connection on the right to the **Waterfall Trail,** which leads down from the campground area.

The **Blackjack Oak Trail** starts or ends near Ferne Clyffe Lake and leads to the main picnic area. The 1-mile trail goes up the side of a hill and can be a bit strenuous, but it offers some nice views of the surrounding terrain and spectacular colors in the fall.

Another must-see trail, the .5-mile **Hawk's Cave Trail,** leads to Hawk's Cave, a large shelter bluff set into a massive set of bluffs. This is an extremely popular trail, especially with children, for the numerous boulders that are found under the shelter bluff and for the many wildflowers and ferns seen along the way.

The **Rebman Trail** is a .25-mile loop near a set of bluffs used by many rappellers. The trail is named for Emma Rebman, who once owned the property, and there is a plaque along the trail honoring her.

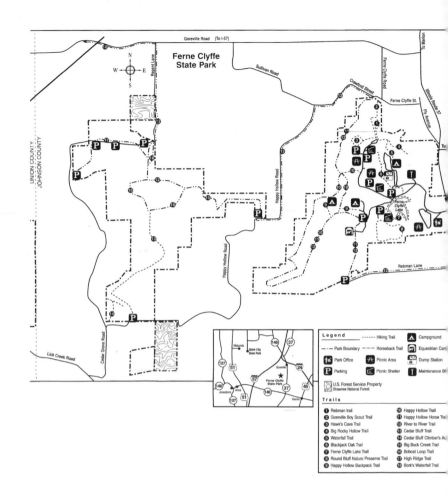

Round Bluff Nature Preserve Trail is one that all visitors should try to experience. The 1-mile trail winds around a sandstone rock bluff, circling a 100-foot knoll where there are some impressive views, particularly at the end of the trail. There are 6 numbered posts corresponding to descriptions in a brochure available at the trailhead of the flora and fauna seen along the trail, including many rare plants, wildflowers, and ferns.

Please note: There are hazardous areas in the park, and the copperhead snake is known to inhabit the area.

REGULATIONS: No motorized vehicles or bicycles permitted on trails. Equestrian use is allowed only on equestrian trails. Swimming and wading are prohibited. Climbing and rappelling permitted in designated areas only.

234   HOURS: The park is open year-round except Christmas and New Year's Day.

DIRECTIONS: From I-57, go east on IL 148 (exit 45) for .6 mile to IL 37. Turn south and follow it for 7 miles to the park entrance on the right side of the road.

CONTACT INFORMATION: Ferne Clyffe State Park, PO Box 10, Goreville, IL 62939; (618) 995-2411; www.dnr.state.il.us/lands/landmgt/parks/r5/ferne.htm

129.   Cache River State Natural Area

HIGHLIGHTS:
- *National Natural Landmark*
- *1,000-year-old bald cypress trees*
- *Wildflowers*
- *State champion cherrybark oak and water tupelo trees*
- *11,249-acre site*
- *2,188 acres of Illinois Nature Preserves (Little Black Slough, Heron Pond, and Section 8 Woods)*
- *Wetlands*
- *Diverse flora and fauna*
- *Floating boardwalk over swamp*
- *Accessible and interpretive trails*

DESCRIPTION: Cache River State Natural Area in Johnson and Pulaski Counties is a remarkable site that contains a mixture of swamps, 1000-year-old bald cypress trees, floodplain forests, primeval tupelos, prairie glades, and the Cache River. Three components comprise the 11,249-acre natural area: Little Black Slough, Lower Cache River Swamps, and Glass Hill. To the west, another large preservation effort is underway to preserve 60,000 more acres of Cache River wetlands. Numerous wildlife species, such as the elusive bobcat, inhabit the area, and various interpretive programs are offered by the Cache River State Natural Area staff. There are more than 18 miles of trails are within the natural area; a few of the short and interpretive trails are described here. A new visitor center is scheduled to open in 2002. Called the Henry N. Barkhausen Cache River Wetlands Center, it will offer various interpretive programs and exhibits.

The 250-foot **Big Cypress Tree Trail** leads visitors to the Lower Cache River, where there is a 1,000-year-old bald cypress tree with a circumference exceeding 40 feet.

The **Lower Cache River Swamp Trail** is 2.5 miles in length; a 1,000-foot, accessible, paved portion leads west along the edge of the Cache River Swamp to an observation platform overlooking the swamp and large bald cypresses. Information signs posted on the observation deck discuss the threatened and endangered species and the Cache River complex.

The **Section 8 Woods Boardwalk Trail and Nature Preserve** leads into a cypress-tupelo swamp and floodplain forest to an observation

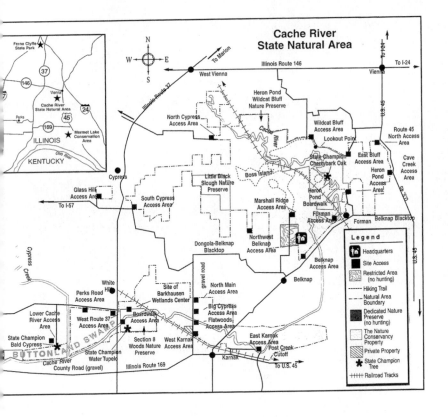

deck where the state champion water tupelo tree may be seen. The wooden boardwalk is 475 feet long.

The **Todd Fink-Heron Pond Trail** is a highlight for visitors to the Cache River State Natural Area. This 1.5-mile interpretive trail leads visitors over the Cache River and Dutchmans Creek past 8 numbered posts corresponding to short descriptions in the trail brochure. The trail parallels the Cache River, and prior to reaching Heron Pond, visitors will see gabions that were installed on the stream bank to prevent erosion. Around 1915, when the Post Creek Cutoff Channel was dug to speed the emptying of water into the Ohio River, it caused the river level to fall and eroded the bank's edge. The trail then leads to a boardwalk that takes visitors into the center of Heron Pond. In the fall, the colors of the foliage on the bald cypresses are impressive. A short walk west of Heron Pond leads to the state champion cherrybark oak tree as well as to other connecting trails.

REGULATIONS: Motorized vehicles, trail bikes, horses, all-terrain vehicles, camping, and fires are prohibited. No collecting or removal of plants, animals, or artifacts permitted within the nature preserves. Leash all pets.

HOURS: The site is open only during daylight for safety.

DIRECTIONS: From I-24, take US 45 south (exit 14) 5 miles past Vienna to Belknap Road. Turn west and go 1.5 miles to Heron Pond Road. Turn right and follow it for .9 mile to the parking area and trailhead. To reach the Big Cypress Tree Trail, take IL 169 west out of Karnak for 1 mile, turning north at the sign for Cypress Access onto the gravel road, and continue for 1 mile to the parking area on the east side of the road. To reach Section 8 Woods, continue south on US 45 (passing Belknap Road) to IL 169, turn west and go 9 miles (passing Karnak) to IL 37. Turn north and travel 1 mile to the parking area on the right side of the road. To reach the Lower Cache River Area, continue .5 mile past Section 8 Woods to Perks Road, turn west, go 1.7 miles to Lower Cache River Road, turn south, and go 1.2 miles to the parking area.

CONTACT INFORMATION: Cache River State Natural Area, 930 Sunflower Ln., Belknap, IL 62908; (618) 634-9678; www.dnr .state.il.us/lands/landmgt/parks/r5/cachervr.htm

130. Lusk Creek Canyon

HIGHLIGHTS:

- *100-foot sandstone canyon*
- *125-acre Illinois Nature Preserve*
- *Lusk Creek Wilderness Area*
- *Lusk Creek, proposed as a Wild and Scenic River*
- *National Natural Landmark*
- *800 plant species, including ferns and mosses*
- *Rock shelters*
- *Native American stone wall*

DESCRIPTION: Lusk Creek Canyon is a 125-acre state nature preserve within the 4,796-acre Lusk Creek Wilderness Area in Pope County. The canyon has unique geological, environmental, and historical features and has been designated a National Natural Landmark, one of 18 in Illinois. The area is home to many rare plants and animals, some found nowhere else in the state. Lusk Creek, a clear, rock-lined stream, has been nominated for designation as a Wild and Scenic River. The canyon area is called Indian Kitchen in reference to a rock shelter that Native Americans once inhabited along the creek.

The 1.25-mile **Indian Kitchen Trail,** across from the parking area, leads to the canyon and nature preserve. At the edge of the canyon is a large horse corral, and a sign is posted on the boundaries of the nature preserve prohibiting horses from entering the nature preserve. The trail leads down to the canyon's edge for a view of the canyon and Lusk Creek. On top of the bluff, visitors may notice a rock wall that was built by Native Americans known as the Woodland people. The purpose of the wall is unclear, although various religious and defensive possibilities have been suggested. A single-lane path leads down the bluff and into the canyon where there is a good view of the canyon walls. Slippery surfaces and steep drops may be encountered, and poisonous snakes such as timber rattlesnakes, cottonmouths, and copperheads are known to inhabit the forest.

REGULATIONS: Stay on trail. All items protected by law. No motorized vehicles allowed. Horses prohibited within the nature preserve.

HOURS: The site is open year-round.

DIRECTIONS: From IL 13 at Harrisburg, take IL 145 south for 18 miles to Eddyville. Turn east on Eddyville Road and proceed .25 mile; turn

View of canyon, Lusk Creek Canyon

left at the sign for Lusk Creek. Follow this gravel road for 1.3 miles to the parking and picnic area on the left side of the road.

CONTACT INFORMATION: Vienna Ranger Station, Route 45N, Vienna, IL 62995; TTY (618) 253-1070 or (618) 658-2111

Shawnee National Forest, 50 Highway 145 S., Harrisburg, IL 62996; (800) 699-6637; www.fs.fed.us/r9/shawnee

131. Millstone Bluff

HIGHLIGHTS:
- *Prehistoric Native American village on top of a bluff*
- *Petroglyphs*
- *Stonebox cemetery*
- *Native American rock wall*
- *Interpretive trail*

DESCRIPTION: On top of 300-foot-tall Millstone Bluff, in Pope County in the Shawnee National Forest, is a Mississippian Indian village with over 20 house depressions, a stonebox cemetery, and petroglyphs inscribed on a flat rock, all unique, historical resources that are protected by law. An interpretive trail constructed by the Forest Service leads the visitor to the top of the bluff, circling the village site. At the trailhead are a few informational boards explaining the history of the Mississippian people as well as the quarrying that has occurred on part of the hill, which can be seen from the parking area. There are wooden stairs near the top of the trail leading to an old Native American stone wall, and the trail then loops around the site past the cemetery, the petroglyphs, and the ruins of various buildings that once stood.

REGULATIONS: Stay on trail. All items protected by law.

HOURS: The site is open daily, 6:00 AM–10:00 PM.

DIRECTIONS: From I-24 near Vienna, head east on IL 146 (exit 16) for .3 mile to IL 147. Turn north and go 11 miles to the entrance on the north side of the road, which is 1.4 miles west of the junction with IL 145.

CONTACT INFORMATION: US Forest Service, 50 Highway 145 S., Harrisburg, IL 62996; (800) 699-6637; TTY (618) 253-1070; www.fs .fed.us/r9/shawnee

132. Limekiln Springs Preserve

HIGHLIGHTS:
- *Limekiln Springs and limestone rock outcrops*
- *Cypress swamp*
- *Cache River floodplain*
- *Wildflowers*
- *Various bird and mammal species, including river otter*
- *Wooden boardwalk*
- *Interpretive trail*

DESCRIPTION: The Limekiln Springs Preserve in Pulaski County is a component of the Cache River wetlands complex owned by the Nature Conservancy in an area of wetlands that various federal, state, and private organizations are restoring cooperatively. Currently, 40,000 acres have been saved, with a goal of acquiring an additional 20,000 acres. The **Limekiln Springs Preserve Trail** is 2-mile dirt path that leads the visitor along the Cache River, the Cache River swamp, and Limekiln Slough, ending at Limekiln Springs. Along the way, it passes through a forest of oak, hickory, maple, beech, ash, and other tree species, as well as various wildflowers. Visitors cross a wooden bridge and a boardwalk to find a bench at the second bridge. There is an interpretive sign at the trail's end near the spring. Many rare and endangered animals may be seen in the area, including the bobcat.

REGULATIONS: Stay on designated trail.

HOURS: The preserve is open only during daylight for safety.

DIRECTIONS: From I-57, head east at the Ullin exit (exit 18) on Shawnee College Road for 2.7 miles to Cache Chapel Road. Turn north and travel 1.1 miles to the parking area on the east side of the road, just prior to the Cache River.

CONTACT INFORMATION: The Nature Conservancy of Illinois, 139 Rustic Cypress Dr., Ullin, IL 62992; (618) 634-2524; nature.org/ states/illinois

Appendix
Selected Bibliography
Index

Appendix: Additional Web Sites

The reader may find the following Web sites, addresses, and phone numbers to be useful sources of information on natural resources, parks, hiking, tourism, and other related items of interest.

American Hiking Society—www.americanhiking.org
1422 Fenwick Lane, Silver Springs, MD 20910; (301) 565-6704

Canal Corridor Association—www.canalcor.org
25 East Washington Street, Suite 1650, Chicago, IL 60602;
(312) 427-3688

Chicago Wilderness—www.chiwild.org

Cypress Creek National Wildlife Refuge—
midwest.fws.gov/cypresscreek
0137 Rustic Campus Drive, Ullin, IL 62992; (618) 634-2231

Illinois Department of Commerce and Community Affairs—
www.commerce.state.il.us
620 East Adams Street, Springfield, IL 62701; (217) 782-7500

Illinois Department of Natural Resources—www.dnr.state.il.us
524 South Second Street, Springfield, IL 62701; (217) 782-6302

Illinois Department of Public Health—www.idph.state.il.us
535 West Jefferson Street, Springfield, IL 62761; (217) 782-4977

Illinois Department of Transportation—www.dot.state.il.us
2300 South Dirksen Parkway, Springfield, IL 62764; (217) 782-7820

Illinois Environmental Protection Agency—www.epa.state.il.us
1021 North Grand Avenue East, Springfield, IL 62702; (217) 782-3397

Illinois Historic Preservation Agency—www.state.il.us/hpa
500 East Madison, Springfield, IL 62701; (217) 785-1511

Illinois Natural History Survey—www.inhs.uiuc.edu
607 East Peabody Drive, Champaign, IL 61820; (217) 333-6880

Illinois Nature Preserves Commission—
www.dnr.state.il.us/inpc/index.htm
524 South Second Street, Springfield, IL 62701; (217) 785-8686

Illinois State Geological Survey—www.isgs.uiuc.edu
615 East Peabody Street, Champaign, IL 61820; (217) 333-4747

Illinois State Museum—www.museum.state.il.us
Spring and Edwards Streets, Springfield, IL 62706-5010; (217) 782-7387

Illinois State Water Survey—www.sws.uiuc.edu
2204 Griffith Drive, Champaign, IL 61820-7495; (217) 244-5455

Midewin National Tallgrass Prairie—www.fs.fed.us/mntp
30071 South State Route 53, Wilmington, IL 60481; (815) 423-6370

National Audubon Society—www.audubon.org
700 Broadway, New York, NY 10003; (212) 979-3000

National Wildlife Federation—www.nwf.org
8925 Leesburg Pike, Vienna, VA 22184; (703) 790-4000

The Nature Conservancy—www.nature.org
4245 North Fairfield Drive, Suite 100, Arlington, VA 22203-1606;
(1-800) 628-6860

NOAA National Weather Service, Central Region—www.crh.noaa.gov

Sierra Club—www.sierraclub.org
85 Second Street, San Francisco, CA 94105; (415) 977-5653

United States Army Corps of Engineers—www.usace.army.mil
441 G. Street NW, Washington, DC 20314-1010; (202) 761-0001

United States Fish and Wildlife Service—www.fws.gov
1849 C Street NW, Washington, DC 20240

United States Geological Survey—www.usgs.gov
12201 Sunrise Valley Drive, Reston, VA 20192

Selected Bibliography

Alesandrini, John. *Field Guide to Mammals of Forest Park.* Peoria: Forest Park Nature Center, 1976.

Benyus, Janine M. *The Field Guide to Wildlife Habitats of the Eastern United States.* New York: Simon & Schuster, 1989.

Bowen, David. *Birds of Illinois.* Bloomington: University of Indiana Press, 1989.

Brown, Vinson. *The Amateur Naturalist's Handbook.* New York: Simon & Schuster, 1992.

Cary, Alice. *Parents' Guide to Hiking and Camping: A Trailside Guide.* New York: W. W. Norton, 1997.

Cornell, Joseph. *Sharing Nature with Children: The Classic Parents' and Teachers' Nature Awareness Guidebook.* 2d ed. Nevada City: Dawn Publications, 1998.

Cowan, Mary Lynn. *Exploring Nature with Children: A Preschooler's Trail Guide to Forest Park Nature Center.* Peoria: Forest Park Nature Center, 1983.

Devore, Sheryl. *Birding Illinois.* Helena: Falcon, 2000.

Griffin, Steven A., and Elizabeth May. *Hiking for Kids: A Family Hiking Guide.* Minocqua: Northwood Press, 1996.

Harris, Stanley E., Jr., William C. Horrell, and Daniel Irwin. *Exploring the Land and Rocks of Southern Illinois: A Geological Guide.* Carbondale: Southern Illinois University Press, 1977.

Hoffmeister, Donald F., and Carl O. Mohr. *Fieldbook of Illinois Mammals.* New York: Dover Publications, 1972.

Illinois Association of Museums and Illinois Historic Preservation Agency. *Directory of Illinois Museums.* Springfield: Illinois Association of Museums and Illinois Historic Preservation Agency, 1999.

Illinois Department of Natural Resources. *A Directory of Illinois Nature Preserves.* Vol. 1, *Northeastern Illinois.* Springfield: Illinois Department of Natural Resources, 1995.

———. *A Directory of Illinois Nature Preserves.* Vol. 2, *Northwestern, Central, and Southern Illinois.* Springfield: Illinois Department of Natural Resources, 1995.

Jeffords, R. Michael, Susan L. Post, and Kenneth R. Robertson. *Illinois Wilds.* Urbana: Phoenix, 1995.

Jones, G. Almut, and David T. Bell. *Guide to Common Woody Plants of Robert Allerton Park.* Champaign: Stipes, 1976.

247

Lawton, Perry Barbara. *Seasonal Guide to the Natural Year: A Month by Month Guide to Natural Events—Illinois, Missouri, and Arkansas.* Golden: Fulcrum, 1994.

Mohlenbrock, Robert H. *Giant City State Park: An Illustrated Handbook.* Springfield: Illinois Department of Conservation, 1981.

———. *Spring Woodland Wildflowers of Illinois.* Springfield: Illinois Department of Conservation, 1980.

———. *Wildflowers of Fields, Roadsides, and Open Habitats of Illinois.* Springfield: Illinois Department of Conservation, 1981.

New Salem Lincoln League. *Lincoln's New Salem: A Village Reborn.* Petersburg: New Salem Lincoln League, 1994.

Penny, James S., Jr. *The Prehistoric Peoples of Southern Illinois.* Carbondale: Center for Archaeological Investigations, Southern Illinois University at Carbondale, 1986.

Phillips, Christopher A., Ronald A Brandon, and Edward O. Moll. *Field Guide to Amphibians and Reptiles of Illinois.* Champaign: Illinois Natural History Survey, 1999.

Prager, Robert G. *Common Spring Wildflowers of Forest Park.* Peoria: Peoria Park District, 1978.

Ranney, Edward. *Prairie Passage: The Illinois and Michigan Canal Corridor.* Prologue by Tony Hiss, essays by Emily J. Harris, and epilogue by William Least Heat-Moon. Urbana: University of Illinois Press and Canal Corridor Association, 1998.

Reader's Digest. *American Nature: Our Intriguing Land and Wildlife.* Pleasantville, NY: Reader's Digest, 1997.

Redd, Jim. *The Illinois and Michigan Canal: A Contemporary Perspective in Essays and Photographs.* Carbondale: Southern Illinois University Press, 1993.

Robinson, Douglas W. *Southern Illinois Birds: An Annotated List and Site Guide.* Carbondale: Southern Illinois University Press, 1996.

Stoles, David W. *Reading For Connections.* Vol. 2, *Creative Exploration of Nature with Young Children.* Milwaukee: Schlitz Audubon Center of the National Audubon Society, 1991.

Sullivan, Jerry. *Chicago Wilderness: A Regional Nature Reserve—An Atlas of Biodiversity.* Chicago: Chicago Region Biodiversity Council, 1999.

Svob, Mike. *Paddling Illinois: 64 Great Trips by Canoe and Kayak.* Madison: Trails, 2000.

Tekiela, Stan. *Birds of Illinois Field Guide.* Cambridge: Adventure, 1999.

Thomas, Benjamin P. *Lincoln's New Salem.* Carbondale: Southern Illinois University Press, 1988.

Vierling, Philip E. *Hiking the Illinois and Michigan Canal and Exploring Its Environs.* Vol. 1, *LaSalle to the Fox River.* Chicago: Illinois Country Outdoor Guide, 1986.

———. *A Self Guided Loop Hiking Trail to the Chicago Portage National Historic Site.* Chicago: Illinois Country Hiking Guide, Vol. 1, No. 1, 1973.

Waldbauer, Gilbert. *The Handy Bug Answer Book.* Detroit: Visible Ink, 1998.

Wiggers, Raymond. *Geology Underfoot in Illinois.* Missoula: Mountain Press, 1997.

Young, Bioloine Whiting, and Melvin L. Fowler. *Cahokia: The Great Native American Metropolis.* Urbana: University of Illinois Press, 2000.

Zyznieuski, Walter G., and George S. Zyznieuski. *A Guide to Mountain Bike Trails in Illinois.* Carbondale: Southern Illinois University Press, 1997.

———. *Illinois Hiking and Backpacking Trails.* Rev. ed. Carbondale: Southern Illinois University Press, 1993.

Index

This index has four parts: alphabetic listings of all sites, accessible trails, interpretive trails, and nature centers.

Walter G. Zyznieuski *(above right)* earned a B.S. degree in geography from Southern Illinois University Carbondale and an M.A. degree in environmental studies from the University of Illinois, Springfield. He has lived and traveled extensively throughout Illinois and has worked for various state and local government entities. A former board member of the Illinois chapter of Rails-to-Trails Conservancy and a founder of the Central Illinois Orienteering Club, he has taught and has led hiking and nature trips for Lincoln Land Community College. His articles and photographs have been published in *Outdoor Illinois, Illinois Parks and Recreation,* and *Public Power.*

George S. Zyznieuski *(above left)* earned a B.S. degree in industrial technology from Illinois State University and now lives in Denver, Colorado, where he owns and operates a business. An avid outdoorsman, he makes frequent visits to his home state of Illinois.

Walter G. Zyznieuski and George S. Zyznieuski are coauthors of *Illinois Hiking and Backpacking Trails* (revised edition) and *A Guide to Mountain Bike Trails in Illinois,* both available from Southern Illinois University Press.